Pray and Play
Dealing with a Fun-Loving Culture

Volume 2 of the Step-by-Step Series
of
Devotional Bible Studies in Bible Contrasts

Bruce Leiter

Author of *Doubtbusters! God Is My Shrink!*
and
*Be Bolder Growin' Older:
Overcoming the Temptations of Old Age*

CrossLink Publishing's Publication
of Volume 1 in the Step-by-Step Series

Pray and Play: Dealing with a Fun-Loving Culture

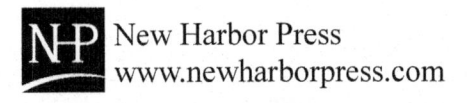

New Harbor Press
www.newharborpress.com

Copyright, © 2015 Bruce Leiter

All rights reserved. No part of this book may be reproduced in any form, except for brief quotations in reviews, without the written permission of the author.

Printed in the United States of America. All rights reserved under International Copyright Law.

ISBN 978-1-63357-009-2

Library of Congress Control Number: 2014954259

Scripture are taken from THE HOLY BIBLE, NEW INTERNATIONAL VERSION®, NIV® Copyright © 1973, 1978, 1984, 2011 by Biblica, Inc.™ Used by permission. All rights reserved worldwide.

A Must Pre-Read: Seven Essential Tips for Reading *Pray and Play*

What is the need for this book? The full title of this book is *Pray and Play: Dealing with a Fun-Loving Culture.* These questions arise: "Why do we need a book about good, clean pleasure? What does God have to do with fun?" I'll deal with the answers to those questions in more detail in this book, but I'll say here that no action is completely neutral. Every thought and activity is spiritual—either done for ourselves, others, or God according to the Bible (see 1 Corinthians 10:31).

As a result, we believers must examine our culture in the light of God's Word, the Bible, and thus evaluate our pleasurable activities in God's light. People in our culture have seldom examined fun from God's point of view. Therefore, we need this book.

Why should I read the whole book? The first chapter contains descriptions and applications of several passages that apply to our approach to pleasure, whereas the remaining chapters apply other parts of the Bible to specific kinds of fun. However, many of the Bible verses can apply to the other kinds of pleasure described here.

Therefore, my advice is that you, dear reader, read through the whole book rather than reading and/or discussing only the kinds of fun in which you are most interested, because other chapters also contain insights and information that will help you.

Where did the idea for this book come from? The background for *Pray and Play* comes from my own experience as a pleasure-lover or hedonist for the first thirty-eight years of my life, twenty-two of those years as a Christian. Those experiences I will describe in this book. Then God used his Word to enable me to examine that area of my life, as I will explain. During the following forty-three years of my life, I have meditated on this subject and tried to put God's Word into practice by his grace alone.

What is the Step-by-Step Series? As the first page says, this book is volume two of the Step-by-Step Series. The first volume is *Be Bolder Growin' Older*, published by CrossLink Publishing, which prepares younger and middle-aged people to avoid the pitfalls of growing older. It also enables older people to find Jesus' victory during that life stage. The whole series, which I hope will have many volumes, invites the reader on a step-by-step journey with Jesus in reading and discussing the Bible as our divine Rescuer's tourist guide toward the goals of spiritual maturity and final perfection. It also deals with the many contrasts in the Bible that may seem to contradict each other but really go together—like praying and playing.

You will encounter several steps of practical application in each book that will help you put the Bible into daily practice on your trip led by Jesus.

What is a devotional Bible study? Individual readers can read all of the books in the Step-by-Step Series for their devotions and personal benefit, but I believe that God led me to design the books with questions for group discussion before each step of practical application. As a result, each book is useful for both personal and group study as a devotional Bible study. A free leader's discussion guide download for this book, with answers for the many discussion questions, is available at my e-mail address: prayandplay7@gmail.com.

Where is our journey with Jesus going? Our terrific tourist trip with our right Ruler follows Paul's path in Philippians 3:10–14, where he uses words about running in the Greek Olympic Games to describe our race toward resurrection perfection when Jesus returns to resurrect our bodies from our graves and to give us final flawlessness in his new creation. The writer to the Hebrews also describes that race in Hebrews 12:1, 2. We run in Jesus' strength with spiritual progress in this life and the goal of final perfection in the next one.

What is the plan of every chapter? Each chapter:

(1) begins with a description of God's unselfish pleasure,
(2) continues with contrasting human selfish pleasure, and
(3) concludes with the fun that God wants believers to experience.

Contents

Chapter One: God's principles about
all pleasurable activities... 1
    A. God's pleasure in believers
    B. The Age of Enlightenment's unbiblical legacy: life as secular *and* sacred
    C. The pursuit of human happiness (hedonism) *versus* divine delight
        1. The pursuit of human happiness (hedonism)
        2. Believers' divine joy
    D. Christians' historical responses to the human emphasis on fun: separatism, and modernism—a biblical middle way
    E. God's delighted desires for believers' lives

Chapter Two: Food 25
Chapter Three: Drinking alcohol 45
Chapter Four: Playing card, video, board games, and the lottery; dancing; moviegoing... 59
Chapter Five: Watching TV and sports, reading books................ 69
Chapter Six: Work and volunteering 85

Chapter Seven: Sex 95

Chapter Eight: Attending professional
and other sports events 103

Chapter Nine: Family events 115

Chapter Ten: Participation sports 129

Chapter Eleven: Use of electronic devices
and the Internet 135

Chapter Twelve: Hobbies, music, and
special interests 147

Chapter Thirteen: Weather 159

Chapter Fourteen: Group worship 173

> Final Part: Jesus' path to God without hedonism,
> separatism, modernism, or secularism

```
        As                                live...
     we                                      to
   travel                                  Jesus
     on                                      in
   Jesus'                                  power
   journey                                  his
   toward                                    us
     our                                   gives
       final                                God
         goal,
```

Chapter One

GOD'S PRINCIPLES ABOUT ALL PLEASURABLE ACTIVITIES

The overall theme of this book

This book's main point is in the meaning of the title. Few people ever think that playing and praying go together. However, God, through the Bible, calls us to combine them.

What are joy and happiness, and how is God involved in them? *Pray and Play* continues the journey with Jesus that began with readers in my book *Be Bolder Growin' Older*. In *Pray and Play*, I apply the Bible's teachings to enjoyable events and activities, so that the final goal of our joy may be the God of the Bible rather than events, objects, and people.

To give you a sneak preview of my approach to the subject of pleasure, I spent January 1, 2014, watching the 100th Rose Parade in Pasadena, California, USA, and the American football bowl victories by Nebraska in the Gator Bowl and Michigan State in the Rose Bowl. By God's grace, I praised him as the divine Creator for his creative power on display in the human creativity and flowery beauty of the parade floats, as well as the coaches' ingenuity and the players' athletic skills in the American football games.

In another example of my approach, I attended a God-honoring graduation ceremony at the Trinity International University in Deerfield, Illinois, USA, in May, 2014. One of the songs was "Jesus, the Very Thought of Thee," with words thought to be written by Bernard of Clairvaux in the A.D. twelfth century . The fourth stanza summarizes the point of this book, "Jesus, our only joy be Thou, as Thou our prize will be; Jesus, be Thou our glory now, and through eternity." I'll let you, dear reader, discern how that hymn shows my message as my book proceeds.

Furthermore, the commencement speech with the title "Seventeen Words That Explain Everything" was based on Psalm 117, "Praise the LORD, all you nations; extol him, all you peoples. For great is his love toward us, and the faithfulness of the LORD endures forever. Praise the LORD." The speaker's main point was that the graduates will find God's blessing in their lives when they lift

God up in all of life. Thus, praising God as the Creator and Rescuer is the path of true joy.

The pattern of each chapter in this book

As a result, let's journey with Jesus' great victory toward dedicating our fun to him by investigating each chapter in the following order,

(1) his perfect pleasure,

(2) selfish, human happiness, and

(3) believers' permanent pleasure in our great God of grace.

God's pleasure in believers

As we reflect on our fun activities, many of us are familiar with God's calls to rejoice in him, but some of us are unaware that God rejoices over believers.

For example, Zephaniah chapter 3 begins with God's right judgment on his people and the world because of their rebellion. The prophet continues in verses 9–13 by describing God's rescue for believers. He then calls all of us to "sing, O daughter of Zion, shout aloud, O Israel! Be glad and rejoice with all your heart, O daughter of Jerusalem! The LORD has taken away your punishment, he has turned back your enemy. The LORD, the King of Israel, is with you; never again will you fear any harm" (verses 14–15).

Then God guides the prophet to make amazing statements in verse 17, "The LORD your God is with you, he is mighty to save. He will take great delight in you; he will quiet you with his love, he will rejoice over you with singing."

Notice that the true God of the Bible is not a distant, emotionless deity, as some people imagine God to be. On the contrary, he feels divine joy about us, his unworthy creatures. Thus, when we rejoice in God as our Creator and Deliverer during our pleasurable events, he returns our joy with his divine pleasure in us.

Furthermore, his message isn't only for Jews, but also for us who trust in Jesus' life, death, and resurrection as our Immanuel ("God with us"—verse 15), because as believers we are "children of Abraham" by faith (Galatians 3 and Romans 4).

My point is that God is not a joyless spoilsport or a killjoy. He feels real joy in blessing true believers.

God's lack of pleasure in unbelievers' death and his pleasure in our repentance

On the other hand, sometimes people have transferred their feelings about overly strict, disciplinarian parents or legalistic relatives to God by imagining that he delights in punishing unbelievers. Other religions have sometimes had that idea, but in Ezekiel 33:11, after God describes Israel's discouragement about their sinful rebellion against him, he pleads with them through the prophet, who is not to be blamed if he warns them about God's judgment for their selfish rebellion: "Say to them, 'As surely as I live,' declares the Sovereign LORD, 'I take no pleasure in the death of the wicked but that they turn from their ways and live. Turn! Turn from your evil ways. Why will you die, O house of Israel?'"

Notice that not only does God feel no joy in punishing sinners, but he also takes pleasure in their turning away from their self-centeredness, an action that he enables them to do. In Luke chapter 15, Jesus also teaches in the parables of the lost sheep, coin, and son (Luke 15:7, 10, 32) that the angels—and presumably God—rejoice when one sinner repents.

Moreover, before God's right punishment of humanity in the universal flood, he doesn't gloat over his vast power to destroy them because of their universal rebellion, but "the LORD was grieved that he had made man on the earth, and his heart was filled with pain" (Genesis 6:6).

I believe that part of God's creation of humans in his likeness and image is that God and humans have emotions in common. His feelings are perfect, but ours are stained with self-centeredness. He grieves as he flawlessly focuses on our good, while we often grieve selfishly.

The source of God's pleasure in us

How can a perfect God rejoice in imperfect humans? In Hebrews 11:5, 6, the writer to the Hebrews shares with us the answer in commenting on Enoch, whose life Moses summarizes in Genesis 5:24: "By faith Enoch was taken from this life, so that he did not experience death; he could not be found, because God had taken him away. For before he was taken, he was commended as one who pleased God. And without faith it is impossible to please God, because anyone who comes to him must believe that he exists and that he rewards those who earnestly seek him."

We must have true faith (that is, a genuine, inner trust in Jesus Christ that shows up as willing obedience in our outward lives, like the way Enoch walks with God) in order for God to be pleased with us.

However, before we get all proud because we have faith in God, we have to realize that other passages like Ephesians 2:8–10 say that our faith is God's gracious gift and that the resulting transformed life is also his work in us through Jesus' victory by the Holy Spirit. As a result, it's Jesus' perfect life and death as our Substitute on the cross that our Father sees when he rejoices in us, because our Judge has stated that we are "not guilty" (that is, justified by the Judge).

Therefore, as we travel with Jesus as the only Path toward our eternal destination, my first point is that God rejoices over his people with a perfect joy. Such a thought should provide us with real, answering, constant joy as we inch along toward our future goal: living forever in his amazing, heavenly presence. Heaven and the new creation must be constant party places!

Bible Discussion Questions:
1. Read Zephaniah chapter 3. What surprises you about this chapter of God's Word? How do you feel about God's rejoicing in you as a believer? Explain.
2. Compare Ezekiel 33:11 and Luke 15:7, 10, 32. Summarize the different human objects of God's sadness and pleasure.

How do you respond to someone who tries to picture God as a distant, emotionless deity? Explain.
3. Read Genesis 6:6. What surprises you about this verse, especially since it precedes God's destruction of the world with a universal flood? Explain. Give other examples of God's justice in the Bible. How does this verse help you understand God's necessary punishment of sin?

* * *

One Step on Our Journey with Jesus: In your prayers, persistently express your joyful praise that God rescued you for eternal joy in his presence and your sorrow for your selfishness.

* * *

An enemy attacking our experience of divine pleasure

In contrast with God's constant, divine joy, humans have substituted other objects of happiness for the true God of the Bible. Instead of following Enoch's walk with God, humanity walks without God partly or completely.

To give you a present example, I just bought a new printer. I don't generally picture my use of the printer as a fun experience, but it's a tool for me to use for my writing ministry, which I do in Jesus' joy. However, the printer's documentation says that it can give you "fun ways to print," "fun filter effects," and "a whole new world of fun." The company plays into our culture's emphasis on secular fun without God.

How did we as North Americans arrive at such a disregard for God? In Allan Turner's Internet article "Christianity: Counterculture Or Subculture?" he writes that in America, instead of a biblical approach, "in our modern topsy-turvy culture, the principal *ism* or system of thought that is being reflected in our creative arts, in our popular literature and music, on our TV screens, in our educational institutions, and even in our churches, is secularism. In secularism, all life, every human value, every human activity must be understood in view of the here and now. There are no windows into the eternal. If there is—and the secularist is either an atheist or agnostic—he [God] is totally irrelevant. All that matters is now."

Just a superficial look at TV programs confirms his observation that secularism has invaded and now controls popular culture that praises human achievement and, by and large, ignores God—except to swear "my God," "Jesus," "Christ," or "hell" meaninglessly to express an emotion. We have totally disregarded God's second commandment: "You shall not take my name in vain." I've even heard professing Christians lacing their words with such language without thinking about it.

As my book proceeds, I hope to propose a Christian approach to our secular culture, but right now I want to explore the source of secular thought.

The roots of secularism go back to the Age of Enlightenment in the late seventeenth and most of the eighteenth centuries leading up to the French and American Revolutions. Wikipedia illuminates us that the Age of Enlightenment is "a cultural movement of intellectuals...emphasizing reason and individualism rather than tradition. Its purpose was to reform society using reason, challenge ideas grounded in tradition and faith, and advance knowledge through the scientific method. It promoted scientific thought, skepticism, and intellectual interchange.... The ideas of the Enlightenment have had a long-term major impact on the culture, politics, and governments of the Western world." I might add that both secularism and the Enlightenment have influenced many Christians' present-day thinking and actions.

Apparently, secular thought peacefully coexisted with biblical thought throughout the eighteenth century but influenced some of the Founding Fathers of the United States, especially Benjamin Franklin and Thomas Jefferson. In fact, the latter founder produced a Bible that excluded all miracles, including Jesus' resurrection.

In the nineteenth century, a Romanticism reaction counteracted secular and Enlightenment thought to emphasize emotion. However, secularism resurfaced in a much more aggressive form in America and Europe in the latter half of the twentieth century and continues in this century. In this form, public expression of faith in God or the Bible is often criticized. Apparently, the idea is that we are to keep our Christian religion to ourselves, while people freely express the religion of secular humanism that centers on human accomplishments without giving any credit to God, the Source of human abilities.

As a result, Christians nowadays need courage to share God publicly, especially in their pleasurable activities, and should expect criticism or silence when they do so. However, people will seldom object when believers share what God has done in their lives and their beliefs based on the Bible, as long as they don't say that the hearers should also believe the same way.

Secular and sacred approaches to life

Eamonn Kelly, in an article entitled "Secular and Sacred" at ftpress.com, says that the separate sacred and secular approaches to life will clash more and more as the twenty-first century proceeds. Religious fundamentalism, he contends, is fighting back against secularism's advance. Such a reaction is not just in Islam, but in every major religion, he asserts.

One 2014 example was the controversy over the patriarch of the popular American TV program *Duck Dynasty* on the A&E network. He disagreed with the homosexual lifestyle as sinful, according to his belief in the God of the Bible, and was promptly suspended by the network.

On the basis of the Bible's clear teaching, I certainly agree with his position and with his USA-constitutionally-protected religious freedom of speech to express his opinions. Interestingly, many people rightly flocked to his defense even though his detractors labeled his comments as "discrimination," just because he was honest about his biblical views. He didn't attack homosexuals but only criticized their lifestyle. That distinction was lost on those who criticized him.

However, because an uproar ensued from people defending his right to free speech, the network reinstated him. After all, money and ratings mean a lot to the USA's TV media.

It seems to me that such controversies clearly illustrate Eamonn Kelly's point that the sacred and secular approaches to public life will battle each other during our time. However, we Christians must always remember that the devil and the demons are our enemies, not humans. They are behind any assault on the Christian faith.

love the sinner, hate the sin?

Ancient and modern love of pleasure

It's time for a comic break.

Some of the members of a health club were having their first meeting. The director of the group said, "Now, I'd like each of you to give the facts of your daily routine."

Several people spoke, admitting their excesses, and then one obviously overweight member said, "I eat moderately, I drink moderately, and I exercise frequently."

"Hmmm?" said the manager. "And are you sure that you have nothing else to add?"

"Well, yes," said the member. "I lie extensively." (comedy.zone.net)

Also, while driving in the American Midwest, I saw a license plate that said, "FUN2B1." I immediately asked, "What 'one'?" My wife couldn't answer my question, as she can't many of my rhetorical inquiries. However, that thought-provoking plate also followed someone's wish, "Enjoy yourselves," a sentiment repeated often in a fun-loving culture.

These examples of human love of pleasure point up the need for Christians to examine our fun in the light of the Bible, God's Word, rather than simply accepting our culture's values.

In addition, these examples illustrate the human weakness in putting other priorities ahead of the importance of maintaining our health and God's gift of a work ethic, which we can also do with joy in our God. Such a tendency to separate activities from God is a danger in a fun-loving culture.

Such a pursuit of pleasure is called hedonism. It is very strong in many cultures, especially in the developed world, where more people have disposable income to spend on pleasures.

For example, when I put the word "hedonism" into dogpile.com, my favorite search engine, I encountered Caribbean resorts by that name. At those expensive places, they brag that they cater to your every "need" for pleasure.

In E. Richard Crabtree's 1960 article, "Secular Threats to Christianity: Hedonism," he writes that hedonism is "the idea that the true goal of life is pleasure, that pleasure is the highest good of man, the guiding principle of human action" (dabar.org).

Crabtree rightly traces back hedonistic love of pleasure through the Greek god of wine, Dionysus (Roman name, Bacchus), to the first person who presented it as a way of life, Aristippus of Cyrene.

However, Crabtree also rightly says that Satan tempted Eve in the Garden of Eden to fall into the sin of pursuing pleasure in rebellion against God in Genesis 3:6, "When the woman saw [because of Satan's temptation] that the fruit was good for food and pleasing to the eye, and also desirable for gaining wisdom, she took some and ate it. She also gave some to her husband, who was with her, and he ate it." Thus, the pursuit of pleasure honored in the American Declaration of Independence as a human right along with life and liberty has been present throughout human history.

John Piper's response to our society's emphasis on fun

Christians have attempted to approach pleasurable activities in different ways.

One recent puzzling approach to hedonism is John Piper's proposal that we can have a "Christian hedonism." According to an article by that name at bcbsr.com, "Piper's argument is basically that God made us to be hedonists and that God himself is a hedonist, but that, for the Christian, our chief source of pleasure or happiness is in God and therefore we should pursue God to achieve our happiness."

However, in a rebuttal to John Piper's curious combination of both the pursuit of pleasure and God at the same website by someone called "Deception In The Church," the writer ably refutes the idea of combining the terms "Christian" and "hedonism" as follows:

"John Piper cannot rewrite the English language." Then the writer goes on to quote the *Webster Dictionary* that the common use of the word "Christian" means "one who professes belief in the teachings of Jesus Christ." On the other hand, he says that "hedonism" means "the doctrine that pleasure or happiness is the sole or chief good in life" and that "one's happiness is the proper goal of all conduct."

True, the Westminster Shorter Catechism question number one says, "What is the chief end of man?" The answer to that first question is: "Man's chief end is to glorify God and to enjoy him forever!" We will enjoy God forever as true believers, but we won't be *pursuing* pleasure, only him.

If a Christian's goal is to follow Jesus, it cannot also be to pursue pleasure. Thus, Piper's curious combination of "Christian" with "hedonism" isn't acceptable. He seems to say that since God pursues pleasure, we should, too. The problem is that nowhere in the Scripture does God reveal that he is a hedonist. He feels joy, and we can share his joy as we follow him, but those facts do not justify the mental leap that he pursues it as a goal, as hedonism seeks to do.

Another Christian response to our culture's emphasis on fun: modernism

Other professing Christians have attempted to blend in with the culture around us by merging it with Christian ideas. The thought is that if our culture thinks it's okay and the Bible doesn't speak clearly against it, we can do it. That emphasis creates an almost-schizophrenic Christianity in which we live secular lives in the world during the week and give God perhaps an hour on Sunday or even that whole day.

Such an approach to fun is unacceptable, because it ignores so many of the Bible's teachings. For example, in Philippians 4:4, God-inspired Paul calls us to "rejoice in the Lord always," not just on the day of worship. Notice that we are to rejoice "in the Lord."

Pray and Play

When we become true believers, God joins our lives to Jesus in a spiritual union "in Christ." Therefore, we must have our enjoyment motivated by and done for Jesus through his resurrection power.

Furthermore, Paul also commands us in 1 Thessalonians 5:16 to "be joyful always."

How can we do our fun to draw our strength from and to honor Jesus? The rest of this book will give you ways to lift up God in your pleasure.

However, we must reject modernism's separation of sacred and secular activities, an emphasis that comes from the Age of Enlightenment.

One more Christian response: separatism

Another response of believers to our culture's emphasis on pleasure is separatism, in which well-meaning Christians separate themselves from the world's fun and label it as sin.

I experienced separatism's negative side when, during my visits in one of my churches, an older man criticized the fact that I owned a TV. He shared with me his near-death experience. When God rescued him and he came home from the hospital, he got rid of his TV as being an evil influence on him and his family.

I accepted his decision as his way of expressing his personal gratitude to God for his gift of more life. However, he continually condemned me during my visits for watching TV. Finally, he said that I wasn't to visit him again. I left him to God because that choice was his to make. However, I find it sad when people's position on such matters separates them from other people.

Another example of separatism is the Amish way of life. I've read a little about their approach to modern life. According to my understanding, the Amish community is extremely important, and we can learn a lot from their cooperation. Apparently, they as a group examine every change as to whether it will harm the community and reject or accept such innovations on that basis.

I admire their peaceful communal life. However, I believe that in order to obey Jesus' command to make disciples of all nations (Matthew 28:16–20), we must have at least some activities and interests in common with unbelievers around us so we can relate to them. Amish people can only evangelize their own children, which they do well by retaining at least 90 percent of them in their communities after letting them go for a couple of years when they are young people.

In the New Testament, separatism is also the Pharisees' approach to their culture that leads to their attempts to control the Jewish nation. Jesus roundly condemns them for their separatist control of others.

As a result, you see that my approach to pleasure is neither to blend in with our secular culture (modernism) nor to separate ourselves completely from the culture around us (separatism). The rest of this book will illustrate what I feel is the Bible's middle way.

Bible Discussion Questions:
1. What evidence of the influence of secularism do you see around you? Give specific examples.
2. How do Christians show the influence of the Enlightenment's separation of secular and sacred activities in their lives? Give examples without naming names.
3. How does hedonism or the love of pleasure show itself in the world around us? In Christians' lives? Give examples without naming names.
4. Give examples of both modernism and separatism other than the ones given by the author. How do you feel about those approaches to pleasure? Explain.

* * *

One Step on Our Journey with Jesus: Confess in prayer the secular or modernist parts of your life. Resolve to pray perseveringly for God's gracious guidance and power through Jesus' triumph to change secular activities, one at a time, into sacred ones or to stop doing them. Tell someone how God changes your life through your prayers.

* * *

Romans 14 and the Bible's approach to fun

Romans chapter 14 presents God's principles about pleasurable pursuits, what the NIV's heading says are "disputable matters." One older man said to me that the passage was about food. Paul may have applied the principles in those verses to food, but the ideas presented there may be applied to many other pleasures.

Let me summarize and apply Paul's ten inspired principles to your pleasurable life:

(1) People who do some kinds of fun should not judge or look down on people who abstain from those pleasures because both belong to Jesus (Romans 14:1–4).

(2) The one who considers every day and all foods equally sacred should accept people who consider one day or one kind of food as more sacred than another. Each doing so should focus on the Lord and give thanks to him (verses 5–7).

(3) Our submission to our divine Ruler in full loving relationship with him should guide us (verses 8–12).

(4) We should not judge, condemn, or look down on our brothers and sisters who act differently in matters not specifically described in the Scripture ("disputable matters"—verse 13a).

(5) Don't invite your fellow Christian to do something that would go against that person's conscience even though you can do it with a clear conscience (verse 13b).

Pray and Play

(6) For someone who considers some food or other fun activity as forbidden even though it's acceptable, like all food, doing it is a sin in that person's life (verses 14–15).

(7) On the other hand, when we do a disputable and pleasurable activity that for us is not wrong, we shouldn't let others criticize us (verse 16). *[handwritten: is ignorance?]*

(8) God's kingdom is about right, peaceful, and joyful living, not primarily about less important disputable matters (verses 17–18).

(9) So let's get along with each other without alienating each other over disputable matters that God does not directly describe in the Bible (verses 19–21). *[handwritten: "not sure matters?"]*

(10) You can do fun activities motivated by faith, like eating and drinking, but if you doubt whether you should be doing any activity, abstain (verses 22–23). *[handwritten: Cause of doubt? the Spirit, fellow Christians]*

You can apply these teachings to all of the activities described in this book.

Paul's further commands in Colossians chapter 2

Another passage that corrects some people's misunderstanding of Paul's teachings in Romans 14 is Colossians 2:13–23, where Paul begins by saying that Christ's resurrection made us alive from the spiritual death of our sinfulness (verse 13). He continues by giving the result of God's forgiveness, since Jesus nails to the cross the rules and regulations of the law that condemns us, and defeats the evil spiritual powers (verses 14 and 15). He advises us to keep others from condemning our food choices or our worship celebrations. All Old Testament commands look forward to Jesus, who fulfilled all of them. Avoid all human rules, since you died with Jesus to the world's control and are part of his one body, the church (verses 16–23).

The writer to the Hebrews' teachings about our faith and fun

Therefore, we give pleasure to God when we do every activity by faith, including our pleasure in him. The writer to the Hebrews holds up Enoch as a "hero of faith" in reference to Genesis 5:22–24, which states that God took Enoch away without his death, "for before he was taken, he was commended as one who pleased God. And without faith it is impossible to please God, because anyone who comes to him must believe that he exists and that he rewards those who earnestly seek him" (Hebrews 11:5b, 6).

Thus, our personal trust in God reflects his pleasure in us back to him, as shown by our loving obedience through our faith in and focus on him in our fun. So party on with Jesus!

David's pleasure in God

One Bible passage, Psalm 16, is David's expression of his joy in focusing on his God. In verse eleven, after David expresses confidence that the grave is not the end of his life (verse 10—a prophecy of Jesus' resurrection), he states, "You have made known to me the path of life; you will fill me with joy in your presence, with eternal pleasures at your right hand." All of us who trust only in Jesus to enable us to be in God's presence after death have unspeakable fun, one continuous party, ahead of us! Such a result is the final goal of our Jesus journey! *[handwritten: Is only in the after-life?]*

Bible Discussion Questions:
1. Read Romans chapter 14. Review the author's ten comments on that passage. Which of those statements do Christians need to put into practice most urgently today? Give your reasons for your choices.
2. Read Colossians 2:13–23. What does Jesus' resurrection have to do with our life? What did his death do for us? How do Paul's teachings apply to your daily life, especially your fun activities? Explain.
3. How does the writer to the Hebrews' description of Enoch's life relate to yours, especially in your pleasurable activities (Hebrews 11:5, 6)? How is God pleased with you? Explain.
4. Read Psalm 16. Describe our life as believers in Jesus after death? What specific verses back up your statement? Explain how you feel about that fact. How are Jesus' death, burial, and resurrection predicted in this psalm? How do those events affect your believing life today? Explain.

* * *

One Step on Our Journey with Jesus: Meditate on one of the ten principles and the corresponding verses from Romans chapter 14 each week for ten weeks. Pray persistently that God will enable you to put

those verses into practice and help you overcome sins related to disobeying them through Jesus' victory.

* * *

Personal experiences that eventually led to the writing of this book

When I was a child, I was bored with the farm and hated farmwork. Then Dad brought home our first TV in 1951 when I was nine years old. (Yes, I just turned seventy-two at this writing.)

Well, that table-model, black-and-white set was my "escape"—mentally, at least—from the drudgery of the farm, as I saw it. We lived north of Chicago, Illinois, and the American baseball Chicago Cubs were on. Thus, I became a TV and sports fanatic. When God made me a Christian seven years later, sports and TV continued as unexamined idols in my life, even into the ministry, until I was thirty-seven years old. I was a believer in God in addition to those unexamined idols that influenced me.

As my idol, sports pretty much controlled my life. For example, when I was a teacher on the southwest side of the Chicago area, I worked summers to pay for our insurances in the fall. As a Fuller Brush salesman walking from house to house, I listened to the afternoon Cub baseball games with my transistor radio by turning my sales case one way between houses, and then shifting the radio's antenna to "turn it off" while I was at the customers' doors. Sports controlled me because I thought about them all day long. It may be hard for you to imagine the loveable loser Chicago Cubs dominating my life, but they did! Perhaps, those of you who are world football or soccer fans and of other sports can relate to my situation.

When I became a pastor in my first church, I preached a message series on the Bible's principles about our use of leisure time, which God used as seeds to help me develop this book thirty years later. In that series, I came to 1 Corinthians 10:31, where Paul tells about disputable matters: "So whether you eat or drink or whatever you do, do it all for the glory of God." After preaching that text, I sensed that God was working in me through my internal dialogue, because I asked myself whether I was watching TV and sports to honor God. I had to answer that I wasn't.

As a result, I had two choices, either to throw both pleasures out like the separatism of the older man in that same church or to find some way to glorify God as I watched sports and TV. I could no longer go on watching with secular pleasure when God confronted me with his Word.

However, as I began to find some way to honor God as I watched TV, I found that I could mentally praise God as the Creator of the human body in sports, and I began looking for TV programs with which I could praise and thank him.

During that process, God set me free from the tyranny of those pleasurable pursuits. My focus during those times God changed from selfish pleasure to God-honoring time in his presence.

Therefore, you can see that I've been meditating on this subject for almost half of my life. I hope that you, my dear reader, can benefit from God's work in my life as we proceed on Jesus' triumphant trek toward his gift of final perfection when he will give us flawless, eternal joy in him.

Now, as I finish writing for the evening, I'm going to praise the divine Creator for his power shown in the human athletic skills in an American basketball game. I will also praise him as the divine Judge for his quality of justice revealed in *Elementary*, a TV program about a modern sleuth, Sherlock Holmes, and his companion, Dr. Watson, who demonstrate God's gifts of human ingenuity and mental capability that outwit evil. That show demonstrates the theme of many American programs that weak human good triumphs over strong human evil, a distinctly biblical idea, too. Sherlock's two weaknesses are addiction to heroin and women.

However, if Sherlock (a male) and the good doctor (a female) ever decide to jump into bed together without getting married first, thus, spoiling their mutual, professional relationship for me, I will stop watching, as I did with another justice drama, *Bones*.

As we joyfully jog with Jesus and each other toward his final kingdom, let's examine...

Chapter Two

Food

People don't have to live very long in the American culture and other developed cultures before noticing that food is a big deal for many people. The following food jokes from food-jokes.com illustrate my point:

Overweight is something that just sort of snacks up on you.

A friend got some vinegar in his ear; now he suffers from pickled hearing.

"I thought you were trying to get into shape."

"I am. The shape I've selected is a triangle."

The snack bar next door to an atom smasher was called "The Fission Chips," a take-off on the British "fish 'n chips."

Why can't you stick (American) food stamps on a letter?

Each day I try to enjoy something from each of the four food groups: the chocolate group, the salty-snack group, the caffeine group, and the 'whatever-the-thing-in-the-tinfoil-in-the-back-of-the-fridge-is' group.

Buffalo meat is getting more popular. I suppose that soon we can expect cold cuts made from it—possibly called "buffaloney."

A restaurant near us has the following saying on their sign during the long, cold, snowy West Michigan winter of 2013/14, "Comfort food for cabin fever," a clever but mistaken slogan that implies that food solves our need for satisfaction. The problem is that such "comfort" is only temporary if we replace God with it or put it alongside of him.

Furthermore, an American Psychological Association survey said that "many people are not coping effectively with stress: People report lying awake (42 percent), overeating or eating unhealthy foods (36 percent) and skipping meals (27 percent) in the past month due to stress...."

However, "unhealthy behaviors like eating and drinking alcohol to manage stress are on a steady decline. Twenty-five percent of Americans report eating to manage stress compared to 34 percent in 2008. Thirteen percent report drinking alcohol to manage their stress compared with 18 percent in 2008" (apa.org, "Impact of Stress").

Thus, the survey reports both good and bad news about Americans' dependence on food due to stress. I'm sure that similar findings would result from surveys in other countries.

God's pleasure in food

We return to Genesis 1:29–31a: "Then God said, 'I give you every seed-bearing plant on the face of the whole earth and every tree that has fruit with seed in it. They will be yours for food. And to all the beasts of the earth and all the birds of the air and all the creatures that move on the ground—everything that has the breath of life in it—I give every green plant for food. And it was so. God saw all that he had made, and it was very good."

Notice that after God's creation and before the humans' rebellion, God gives all beings plants to eat, not animals. As a result, we might want to avoid eating meat, except that after the flood, God also says to Noah as the new head of humanity, "Everything that lives and moves will be food for you. Just as I gave you the green plants, I now give you everything" (Genesis 9:3).

However, my point is that God cares about our food. Obviously, our Father-Creator—in spite of some people's belief that he has a human body—"is spirit, and his worshipers must worship him in spirit and truth," according to Jesus (John 4:24).

On the other hand, Jesus eats broiled fish and shows his nail-scars in his resurrected human body to demonstrate that he still has his human body, now perfected. Someday, we believers will be like him when he returns.

Furthermore, in Matthew 22:1–14, Jesus' parable compares the kingdom of heaven to a king's wedding banquet for his son's marriage. The invited guests refuse to come to the banquet, a shocking action in that culture. As a result, the king invites anyone else who will come. However, he punishes a wedding guest who comes without wedding clothes with eternal banishment by telling his servants to "tie him hand and foot, and throw him outside, into the darkness, where there will be weeping and gnashing of teeth" (Matthew 22:13).

Jesus comments on his parable, "For many are invited, but few are chosen" (verse 14).

Therefore, his main point is that he condemns the religious leaders' rejection of him and other people's lack of true faith and seems to imply that our next life will be one continuous banquet. However, it's dangerous to take every detail of a parable literally. As far as I'm concerned, the jury is still out about whether we will be eating at all in the next world. Perhaps Jesus teaches us that he is our eternal "banquet" by supplying our satisfaction forever.

However, Jesus clearly says that we had better be ready for his Second Coming, wearing his perfect "clothes," and that he is the perfect Satisfier of all of our needs in this life and the next.

Jesus as the bread of life in John's gospel

That Jesus himself satisfies our deepest needs is his point in John 6:35, 53–55, "I am the bread of life. He who comes to me will never go hungry, and he who believes in me will never be thirsty….I tell you the truth, unless you eat the flesh of the Son of man and drink his blood, you have no life in you. Whoever eats my flesh and drinks my blood has eternal life, and I will raise him up at the last day. For my flesh is real food and my blood is real drink."

Some people have taken Jesus literally by saying that the Holy Communion bread and grape drink somehow change into Jesus' literal body and blood. However, all of Jesus' "I am" statements in John's gospel are metaphors comparing actual, physical objects or people to the spiritual reality we have in Jesus. For example, when Jesus compares himself to the gate of a sheep pen in John 10:7, he says that he is the only way to come under his eternal care and protection as the good Shepherd, thus, identifying with the comforting imagery of God as the good Shepherd of Psalm 23. Also, Jesus says that he gives believers "living water," the Holy Spirit, to give us constant spiritual satisfaction for our "thirst" for him (see John chapter 4).

In other words, Jesus, in all of his "I am" comparisons in John's gospel, claims to be the "I AM THAT I AM" God of the burning bush in Exodus three and four, just as his heavenly Father is, and to be the only complete satisfaction for all of our needs as God's adopted children.

However, he also claims, "I and the Father are one" (John 10:30). God is three Persons in one God. I invite you to read through the Gospel of John to see that amazing, mysterious truth displayed clearly, if you doubt it. (I refer you also to my first book, *Doubtbusters! God Is My Shrink!* for a discussion of the 3-in-1 God and other biblical truths.)

In addition, in John chapter 6, Jesus feeds a good-sized small town of 5,000 men plus women and children—for a total of about 12,000 people—with a few fish and loaves of bread; compares himself favorably with Moses' manna, God's miraculous bread on which Israel thrived while wandering forty years in the desert; and then compares himself to the nourishment of bread as his present and future provision for our eternal lives through our true faith in him.

As a result, Jesus' comparison of himself to bread cannot be taken literally but is nonetheless rich in figurative meaning.

A popular Italian restaurant near us has this slogan: "There is no love more sincere than the love of food." I respectfully disagree that we must love our food. That message sounds like "foodaholism," my made-up word, meaning that food is the source of our pleasure.

On the other hand, if we trust in Jesus as our Food for life that will last forever, we can then enjoy our fellowship with him and other people as we eat his gift of physical food. Which type of food do you love more?

Does God eat Israel's Old Testament sacrifices?

One large religious group, the Mormons or the Church of Jesus Christ of Latter-day Saints, has wrongly imagined God to be an enhanced human being who lives in outer space and gained the status of being God. They will not tell you these teachings by Joseph Smith when they come to your door, but former Mormons have enlightened us that the Mormon leaders actually believe this fanciful tale.

God will judge them, but we find help in Psalm 50:7–15 to evaluate the incorrect thoughts that God is a superhuman person.

First of all, you need to understand that the pagan peoples around ancient Israel believe that their gods selfishly create humans in order to feed them. As a result, their sacrifices are for that purpose. It's clear that the false gods are merely larger-than-life humans with the same appetites as people. However, behind all of false gods in any era are the evil spirits (demons). That same comment can also be made about the Greek and Roman gods of the New Testament era.

Second, in contrast to imagined false gods, the true God says in Psalm 50:13–15, "If I were hungry I would not tell you, for the world is mine, and all that is in it. Do I eat the flesh of bulls or drink the blood of goats? Sacrifice thank offerings to God, fulfill your vows to the Most High, and call upon me in the day of trouble; I will deliver you, and you will honor me."

Thus, Israel's slaughtered animals are their thankful offerings to supply the needs of the full-time priests and Levites who serve God by leading the people in worship. Moreover, the blood shed and the lives given by those animals on the altar at the place of worship look forward to the perfect God-man Lamb, who offers himself to satisfy God's justice in punishing human rebellion for all who trust only in Jesus' sacrificed body and blood shed on the cross.

The bottom line is that God the Father doesn't have a human body to eat food but does rejoice, in a perpetual party, about our coming to him by faith and our increasing trust in him.

That biblical fact is the reason I tend to think that the banquet comparisons in the Bible are figurative ways to describe our eternal joy and satisfaction with Jesus in the next world. However, I guess that we'll find out someday when Jesus returns, won't we?

Bible Discussion Questions:

1. Why do you suppose that food has such importance in many cultures? Explain.
2. Why do so many people let stress affect whether they eat more or less food? What are your favorite foods? Why?

3. Read Genesis 1:29–31 and 9:3. What conclusion do you make about God's provision of food based on these texts? Why?
4. Read Matthew 22:1–14 and John 6. What, in your own words, is Jesus' teaching about food in these passages? What practical conclusions do you make about your present and future life from these passages? Why?
5. According to the previous passages and Psalm 50, what teachings does God's Word make about his divine nature? Explain.

* * *

One Step on Our Journey with Jesus: Praise your heavenly Father's amazing nature as spirit and Jesus' human and divine natures in one Person at the beginning of your prayers. Thank the true, 3-in-1 God for the Holy Spirit's gift of faith.

* * *

Human pleasure in and exaggeration of food's importance

We humans tend to exaggerate food's importance. Take, for example, the following excerpts from food-jokes.com:

Moments before a famous Shakespearean actor was to perform Hamlet to a packed house in New York, he dropped dead. The house manager solemnly went onstage and announced, "We are sorry to bring you this news, but our performance tonight has been canceled due to the untimely demise of our featured performer."

From the back of the theater, a voice cried out, "Give him some chicken soup!"

Startled, the stage manager cleared his throat and replied, "I apologize if in my grief I have not made my solemn message clear. The man is deceased."

Once again, but more emphatically, the voice rang out, "Give him some chicken soup!"

Having had about enough, the manager bellowed back, "Sir, the man is dead. Giving him chicken soup couldn't possibly help."

To which the voice replied, "It couldn't hurt!"

The human mistake satirized here is to assume that food can cure all human ills without any reference to the true God, who can use food, exercise, and medical means to bless us with a good measure of health.

The following joke on food-jokes.com also shows exaggerated human pleasure in food and drink: "I am passing this on to you because it was passed on to me and has definitely worked for me. By following the simple advice I read in an article, I have finally found inner peace. It read: 'The way to achieve inner peace is to finish all the things you've started.' I looked around to see all the things I started and hadn't finished … So far today I have finished one bottle of vodka, a bottle of red wine, a bottle of Scotch, some Valium, a large box of chocolates, and nine beers. You have no idea how good I feel. You may pass this on to those you feel are in need of Inner Peace." If you think that God's inner peace really comes in this way, read Philippians 4:6, 7. Follow God's instructions through Paul persistently, instead of this joker's advice, to have God's real, permanent inner peace.

Paul's inspired advice about food

The Bible also describes God's estimate of human selfish pleasure in Philippians 3:18, 19 as follows: "For, as I have often told you before and now say again even with tears, many live as enemies of the cross of Christ. Their destiny is destruction, their god is their stomach, and their glory is in their shame. Their mind is on earthly things." In this way, inspired Paul describes the sad, unbelieving human condition that replaces the true Object of our desires with food and other earthly things.

In addition, Paul addresses some Corinthian Christians' eating food that is sacrificed to the Greek false gods by writing in 1 Corinthians 8:8, 9, "We know that an idol is nothing at all in the world and that there is no God but one....But not everyone knows this. Some people are still so accustomed to idols that when they eat such food they think of it as having been sacrificed to an idol, and since their conscience is weak, it is defiled. But food does not bring us near to God; we are no worse if we do not eat, and no better if we do."

However, Paul continues by warning his readers not to eat what others consider to be sinful and not to invite them to eat it, too, since those actions would draw those people into violating their conscience and making them sin. (See Romans 14.)

One conclusion that we can draw is that God gave us food to bless us with health, not for comfort from stress. Only Jesus is the Food of life, especially eternal life, not our stomach gods.

In another passage (1 Timothy 4:1–5), Paul describes certain unbelievers as telling people to "abstain from certain foods," probably unclean foods forbidden in Leviticus chapter 11, "which God created to be received with thanksgiving by those who believe and who know the truth. For everything God created is good, and nothing is to be rejected if it is received with thanksgiving, because it is consecrated by the word of God and prayer."

First of all, God inspires Paul to say that the national form of the law for Israel about unclean foods disappears through Jesus Christ's death, whereas we still need his cleansing for our inner and outer sinful uncleanness. Second, God calls us through Paul to pray thankfully for his gifts of health and strength as we eat his gift of food. Third, I firmly believe that if we pray for God's blessing on our food in order to live selfish lives, he will not hear our prayers. Fourth, God wants us to use food to honor him with the energy that he gives us through it. Such a motive should be our purpose for praying before meals, and real fellowship should be the content of our meal times.

Adam and Eve's food temptation

We return to the beginning of human idolatry. In Genesis 3:6, inspired Moses describes Eve's temptation in response to Satan's untruths: "When the woman saw that the fruit of the tree was good for food and pleasing to the eye, and also desirable for gaining wisdom, she took some and ate it." At the very point that humanity teeters on the brink of disaster, Eve desires to use God's good food selfishly by trying to be equal with God, her Creator.

Since then, humanity has believed in Satan's falsehood that we can gain lasting comfort from food. Eve tries to climb up to God by eating the forbidden fruit but falls with her husband to the depth of God's rightful banishment from his powerful presence. We can only re-enter his presence through faith in the God-man Jesus, the Food of life.

Bible Discussion Questions:
1. What does Philippians 3:6, 7 tell you about how to gain God's gift of inner peace? How can you put this passage into practice? Explain.
2. What evidence have you observed that confirms Paul's teaching in Philippians 3:18, 19? Give examples.
3. Read 1 Corinthians 8:8, 9. How does Paul contradict our culture's emphasis on "comfort" foods? Explain.
4. Read 1 Timothy 4:1–5. With what attitudes and prayers should we approach eating food? Why?
5. How will this chapter on food change your attitudes and actions with food? Give specific examples.

* * *

One Step on Our Journey with Jesus: Resolve to pray for God's gift of self-control, one of the fruits of his Holy Spirit (Galatians 5:23), to enable you to use food as his means of giving health, instead of the human impulsiveness that seeks comfort from food. When God gives you the victory of self-control, tell believers and unbelievers around you about his blessing, always giving him the credit.

* * *

Personal experience with chocoholism

"Hello, my name is Bruce, and I am a chocoholic." My introduction would be like that one at an imagined Chocoholics Anonymous (CA) meeting. Yes, I have a chocolate gene in my DNA.

How does one deal with constant craving for chocolate biblically? Well, the Bible is clear that we are called to crave only God, but the human race has replaced him with earthly objects of our affection. However, moderate amounts of chocolate are good for a person's health.

I believe that God guided me to the following approach.

First of all, since chocolate in moderate amounts is beneficial for us, I take one daily dose at lunchtime—that is, one layer of chocolate-covered peanuts or nuts, a broken-up part of a chocolate candy bar, *or* peanut M&Ms and a layer of nuts (also very good for me) on the bottom of a very small margarine cup. Thus, God has taught me to have joy in him and his gift of health during lunch.

Second, while I swim a half hour of laps at a swimming pool five afternoons a week, I pray—among other petitions—for Jesus' divine powerful victory in his life, death, and resurrection to replace with the Holy Spirit's fruit of self-control (Galatians 5:22, 23) my eating impulsiveness and other ways when that old nature quality shows up in my life. God has answered that daily prayer and my other prayers all day long by enabling me to give up all between-meal snacks to maintain a steady, normal weight and to stay away from chocolate at other times than lunch, except to have some chocolate once in a while for dessert at supper.

In this way, God has taught me to "pray and play" with my food to honor him with his gift of health. It's all to his credit.

Jesus' blessing on believers' hunger for him

On our terrific trip to Jesus' final destination, we investigate the object of true believers' hunger with one of Jesus' amazing beatitudes in Matthew 5:6, "Blessed are those who hunger and thirst for righteousness, for they will be filled." God's great blessing of eternal satisfaction comes to people who desire to conform themselves to God's divine nature and right ways.

Of course, when God gives us true faith through Jesus' life, death, and resurrection by the Holy Spirit's power, he as our Judge declares us right with him and not guilty—God's gift of declared right standing for a lifetime of failures.

However, we then face a whole life of increasingly right living in practice. I believe that Jesus refers in the beatitude to that practical obedience gradually growing in our lives as we read the Bible, hear it proclaimed and taught, and as we pray. Thus, only God can satisfy our hunger for increased right living.

The whole unbelieving human race looks in the wrong places—such as food, objects, and people—to satisfy their hunger and thirst, which are desires that only God can permanently fulfill.

For example, during the last day of the Feast of Tabernacles, when the priests carry water from the Pool of Siloam to the Temple's altar to celebrate God's miraculous gift of water for Israel in the Sinai desert, Jesus shouts in John 7:37, 38, "'If anyone is thirsty, let him come to me and drink. If anyone believes in me, as the Scripture has said, streams of living water will flow from within him.' By this, he meant the Spirit, whom those who believe in him were later to receive."

Again, Jesus contrasts the temporary nature of the water that God miraculously gives to the Israelites during their wandering in the arid area between Egypt and the Promised Land with his permanent provision to slake their thirst eternally.

He makes a similar promise to the Samaritan woman at Jacob's well in John 4:13, 14: "Everyone who drinks this water [that you get here] will be thirsty again, but whoever drinks the water I give him will never thirst. Indeed, the water I give him will become in him a spring of water welling up to eternal life."

God's principles for eating food and for all actions

In 1 Corinthians 6:12–13a, Paul quotes and answers the Corinthians' misstatements about their Christian freedom, "'Everything is permissible for me,' but not everything is beneficial. 'Everything is permissible for me'—but I will not be mastered by anything. 'Food for the stomach and the stomach for food'—but God will destroy them both. The body is not meant for sexual immorality, but for the Lord, and the Lord for the body."

The following important ideas come to us here from God: first, do only what benefits you and others; second, don't let anything control you (true self-control only comes from God); third, both eating food with selfish pleasure and engaging in sex outside of marriage are outside of God's will; and fourth, only the 3-in-1 God himself can satisfy our longing for fulfillment, not food or sex.

In 1 Corinthians 10:31, Paul presents God's principle for all actions, including eating food: "So whether you eat or drink or whatever you do, do it all for the glory of God." Here, Paul gives people the precious principle that in doing all actions for other people's good, we also seek to honor God for his glory (honor) as our motive. In eating food, we must consciously lift God up, thankfully, in seeking his gift of health to show our love to him, since he is the Creator and Provider of our nourishment.

We can apply his principle, as with many Bible passages, to all of the pleasurable pursuits in this book. Therefore, we need to make sure that we are pursuing God during fun activities, because other objects of our pleasure are only temporary in their ability to satisfy us.

God's opinion of fasting

In Isaiah chapter 58, God speaks through the prophet about Israel's selfish abstinence from food on a day of fasting. He says that his people show him outward reverence by denying themselves food but nevertheless act unlovingly.

God goes on, "Is not this the kind of fasting I have chosen: to loose the chains of injustice and untie the cords of the yoke, to set the oppressed free and break every yoke? Is it not to share your bread with the hungry and to provide the poor wanderer with shelter—when you see the naked, to clothe him, and not to turn away from your own flesh and blood?" (Isaiah 58:6, 7). Thus, outwardly pious abstinence from food and other religious observances mean nothing when our use of food and all of his gifts is selfish.

What will God's blessing be when we give our food to him to be a blessing to others with his gift of health and share our wealth with those who have less? "Then your light will break forth like the dawn, and your healing will quickly appear; then your righteousness will go before you, and the glory of the LORD will be your rear guard. Then you will call, and the LORD will answer; you will cry for help, and he will say: Here am I" (verses 8–9). As a result of our unselfish use of food and our other resources to give God credit for his blessings, he will bless us abundantly.

It is my understanding that the Bible doesn't command us to abstain from food, but I've known Christians whom God has blessed abundantly through fasting, which he can use to focus us on him.

On the other hand, an unhealthy abstinence from food is the vicious disease of anorexia, in which mostly young women imagine themselves to be fat and therefore skip meals to "get thinner." That vicious disease seems to stem from a perfectionism that attempts to be like the Barbie doll. Such a disease needs medical and psychological help.

"Don't play with your food."

My mother and a lot of moms would say, "Don't play with your food!" I say, on the basis of the Bible, "Eat with your pleasure in the true God and his goodness in feeding you!"

Bible Discussion Questions:

1. Read Matthew 5:6 in its context. How do you think this verse fits with the rest of the beatitudes? How can we put Jesus' teaching in this verse into practice so that God's promised blessing will come to us more? Explain.
2. Read John 4:13–14 and 7:37–38 with the surrounding verses. How can we get God's gift of "living water"? What difference does such a Gift make in our lives? Why can't we get him in our own strength? Explain.
3. Read the contexts of 1 Corinthians 6:12–13 and 10:31. How can God change believers' lives by way of these verses? Explain.
4. Read Isaiah chapter 58, especially verses 6–9. How do you feel about fasting from food for a period of time to focus on God, for example, during Lent? What is God's point about Israel's fasts? What does this passage say about our religious ceremonies, especially our group worship? Explain.

* * *

One Step on Our Journey with Jesus: Pray before and after your meals with genuine thankfulness to the Creator, who has given you food for your nourishment, health, and strength. Thank him for the fellowship that he enables you to have with friends and family while eating food. Then dedicate your health in committed love to him through Jesus'

triumph. As God gives you spiritual progress in this area, share God's work in your life with someone else.

* * *

As we tread our triumphant trail with Jesus toward our final goal, let's find God's will for...

Chapter Three

DRINKING ALCOHOL

God's pleasure in his people's future return

The prophet Amos is a Judean farmer from the south, whom God calls to preach his Word in northern Israel. In Amos chapter 9, God announces his judgment of Israel because they wander after false gods. Then God promises to restore Israel: "The days are coming," declares the LORD, "when the reaper will be overtaken by the plowman and the planter by the one treading the grapes. New wine will drip from the mountains and flow from the hills. I will bring back my exiled people Israel; they will rebuild the ruined cities and live in them. They will plant vineyards and drink their wine; they will make gardens and eat their fruit" (Amos 9:13–14).

Notice several features of this prophecy:

(1) This passage has yet to be fulfilled in Israel's life, since Assyria exiled them in 712 B.C. The northern part of Israel where Amos preached never returned to the Promised Land. In fact, no one heard from them again.

(2) In just about every translation, the translators rightly put these verses in poetic form. Thus, wine flowing from the hills poetically pictures our powerful Parent's perfect provision of abundant blessings that produce his people's perfect joy in him in a future, perfect world.

(3) Prophecies almost always have direct and deeper meanings. The direct meaning, I believe, is that some of the "northerners" would flee to southern Judah when Assyria deports the rest of the northern ten tribes somewhere in northern, present-day Iraq.

(4) Therefore, the northern Israelites who defect to Judah would leave the land with the rest of the southerners when Babylon forces them to go to present-day, far southern Iraq about 586 B.C. Some of their families would return to the land seventy years later, thus, directly fulfilling Amos's prophecy.

(5) Of course, the deeper meaning of a perfect paradise for our Provider's people has yet to happen. The Book of Revelation (21:1) glimpses a future new heaven and new earth, a perfect paradise. In that chapter, God's new Jerusalem, a symbolic picture of God's people from Israel and all nations, descends toward the new earth.

(6) Amos's figurative picture of a flood of wine in Israel does not show God's approval of drinking too much alcohol. It instead

shows God's pleasure in blessing his people with sober joy in him. However, Amos quotes God as observing that the restored people will drink wine and eat the fruit from their orchards, a figurative picture of God's lavish plenty and satisfaction in his covenant people's lives.

(7) Finally, New Testament passages (Romans 4, Galatians 3, and Ephesians 2) clearly say that all believers in Jesus Christ are children of Abraham and part of God's people, the church. Therefore, Amos' prophecy is for all who trust only in Jesus as our Road and Escort to God the Father's heavenly ruling place, the goal of our earthly journey.

Jesus' miracle of turning water into wine

Furthermore, in a well-known New Testament passage (John 2:1–11), Jesus attends a wedding at which people are imbibing in great amounts of wine. He miraculously turns large jars of water into wine when they run out. Of course, his attendance at the wedding where people are probably getting drunk doesn't mean that he condones people's drunkenness. (On the other hand, in his day, people grew up drinking wine. As a result, they could tolerate more alcohol than people of Western cultures. But they still could get drunk, a condition against which Paul warned.)

However, Jesus demonstrates that he is the Creator of earthly drink with his heavenly Father, a point that he makes clear to the Samaritan woman two chapters later, when he offers her living water. John's inspired point is that such a divine human Rescuer is worthy of our faith.

A government's information about alcohol

As we turn to human pleasure caused by alcohol, we turn to the Michigan (USA) Drivers Safety Test, which states, "Most people who drink, drink to relax or have 'fun.' This is called recreational drinking. Drinking in excess or frequently to obtain the side effects of alcohol is classified as alcohol abuse. [Another] reason for drinking is classified as 'experimentation,' which is typically associated with teenagers who have not yet experienced the effects of alcohol on their own system. Unfortunately, most people have a limited knowledge about alcohol and how it impacts their judgment and health. Regardless of the reason, the effects of alcohol are unpredictable."

Earthly attempts at humor about alcohol

The following "jokes" show our culture's fixation on using alcohol for "fun" (edited from jokes4us.com):

- Q: What is a man's idea of a balanced diet?
- A: A Budweiser in each hand!
- Q: You know what's fun about being sober?
- A: Nothing.
- Q: What has eight arms and an IQ of 60?
- A: Four guys drinking Bud Light and watching a football game!
- Q: How can you find the guy who drank a case of Coors Light?
- A: He's the one dancing like a fool!
- Q: How does a man show he's planning for the future?

A: He buys two cases of Miller Lite instead of one.
Q: What is the difference between a sofa and a man watching (American) Monday Night Football?
A: The sofa doesn't keep asking for Bud Light!
Q: Where do monkeys go to drink?
A: The monkey bars!

Boy: "I love you so much, I could never live without you."
Girl: "Is that you or the beer talking?"
Boy: "It's me talking to the beer."

"Alcohol doesn't turn people into somebody they're not. It just makes them forget to hide that part of themselves."

"Alcohol is never the answer … But it does make you forget the question."

"A man's got to believe in something; I believe I'll have another drink."

"My doctor told me to watch my drinking, so now I drink in front of a mirror."

I strongly disagree with the second attempt at humor in the list above. Being sober in God involves lots of fun centered on him, as I hope you discover throughout my book!

I only include these "jokes" because they demonstrate the denying, addictive behavior of people's excessive alcohol use, and because they are somewhat creative, not because I have chuckled at any of them. I believe that excessive alcohol use and the establishments promoting that behavior are far from funny; rather, they are sad. I refused to watch the old American TV series *Cheers* because taverns are too often the places for people's escape from reality into a dreamland of fantasy rather than places where they face reality.

Recently, I saw a bar's advertising sign that bragged about their happy hour: "Longest Happy Hour—3 P.M. to 7 P.M." I wondered to myself how people could possibly be happy the other twenty hours of the day and whether a quadruple happy hour would make a person four times as happy.

The problem with alcohol addiction, as with any addiction, is that we generally don't know how much is too much. The father of lies, Satan, deceives people into denying that they have had more than they can handle. In fact, some people can't handle any alcohol at all. Others get drunk seemingly without any bad physical results. The problem, however, is that their minds are impaired and that they lose good judgment. For that reason alone, people should never drink and drive, unless they drink nothing stronger than water or soft drinks.

Rather than our escape from life through alcoholic beverages, God wants us to enjoy him at the center of our fun life. Such enjoyment is much deeper and higher than any superficial highs caused by alcohol.

Personal experiences with wine and beer

In the mid-1960s on New Year's Eve, we celebrated the changing of the year with relatives when they offered me a glass of wine. Since I had nothing against a little wine, which Paul recommended to Timothy for his stomach problems (1 Timothy 5:23), I accepted their offer. The drastic result was a huge respiratory reaction to the wine that made me abstain from alcoholic beverages ever since then.

However, at one point on a hot summer day in the late '60s, someone offered me a beer. I sipped a little and hated its taste. Even when we went to Wrigley Field to watch the Chicago Cubs play baseball, we ate lunch or supper outside the ballpark; each of us only bought one item in the park because of the park's high prices. Beer was never on our menu; its smell even repels me.

These two experiences are the sum total of my alcohol consumption for seventy-two years. They weren't very pleasant ones. Therefore, I have never connected alcohol with sports events the way some people do.

Bible Discussion Questions:

1. What are your reactions to the alcohol "jokes" and the author's comments about drinking? Please explain.
2. Read Amos chapter 9, especially verses 13 and 14. Which of the author's seven comments strike you as helpful? Make you hopeful? Why?
3. Read John 2:1–11. What parts of this passage puzzle you? Which parts of these verses help your faith grow as John intended them to do?

* * *

One Step on Our Journey with Jesus: Identify qualities in your life that God wants you to remove

and the corresponding qualities that God wants to increase in you. Pray persistently to God, through Jesus' life and death, for the removal of your old nature. Also, pray that God, through Jesus' resurrection, will add the corresponding new nature qualities to your life. If you have a problem with alcohol, admit it and pray persistently for God's wisdom as you abstain from it or use small amounts of it. Also, get help from God through others at Alcoholics Anonymous or similar organizations.

* * *

God's created gifts and the human response of selfish pleasure

Psalm 104 is a hymn of praise to God as the Maker of all creation and the Provider of many good blessings for human work and pleasure. For example, in verses 14 and 15, the inspired writer commends God's ongoing work as follows: "He makes grass grow for the cattle and plants for man to cultivate—bringing forth food from the earth: wine that gladdens the heart of man, oil to make his face shine, and bread that sustains his heart." Thus, wine, oil, and bread are our Creator's gifts.

However, God's fallen humanity has made God's good gifts into the objects of our desire rather than God, who gave them to us. Thus, we rebels have sought selfish comfort and escape through food and drink.

Therefore, God's Word also points out people's self-centered abuse of God's blessings. For example, Solomon writes in Proverbs 20:1, "Wine is a mocker and beer a brawler. Whoever is led astray by them is not wise."

As the Proverbs and Psalms demonstrate, God's gift of true wisdom is a believer's ability to apply God's will as described in all of the Bible to daily life. When we let food or drink control us and leave God out of the picture, we lack wisdom and discernment to honor him as our Provider.

In addition, the writer of Ecclesiastes, probably Solomon, describes all human events and accomplishments "under the sun" or "under heaven" as "meaningless." Those phrases refer to his attempts to experience many accomplishments without God. As a result, he concludes that life without God is like a breath that disappears quickly, the literal meaning of the word "meaningless." At the beginning of chapter 2, he writes, "I thought in my heart, 'Come now, I will test you with pleasure to find out what is good. But that also proved to be meaningless. 'Laughter,' I said, 'is foolish. And what does pleasure accomplish?' I tried cheering myself with wine and embracing folly—my mind still guiding me with wisdom. I wanted to see what was worthwhile for men to do under heaven during the few days of their lives" (Ecclesiastes 2:1-3). The writer's conclusion is that selfish human activity, especially drinking alcohol, is short-lived, empty, and therefore lacking in permanent value.

Thus, we can ask: what lasting benefit comes from self-centered overindulging in alcohol and food? Not one.

However, moderate use of food and drink centered on joy in believers' divine Source has eternal value.

Believers' pleasure compared to selfish pleasure in drinking too much

God, through Paul, calls getting drunk a sin. "Do not get drunk on wine, which leads to debauchery. Instead, be filled with the Spirit" (Ephesians 5:18). In other words, don't fill yourself with alcoholic "spirits," but instead seek God's filling with the Holy Spirit.

Drinking too much alcohol, like illegal drugs, creates the illusion of human happiness, a high from which we always come down. Such an upper is very temporary, so that those who think they "need" its human high have to produce it over and over again.

By contrast, when God, through the Holy Spirit, baptizes us the first time, he stays with us forever, slowly growing in influence over our rebellious nature. The Holy Spirit from our Father, through Jesus' death and resurrection, produces in us the amazing miracle of the new birth. He re-makes us to be something like a new baby hungry for the Creator. How?

Notice in 1 Peter 1:23, after the writer calls Christians to love one another genuinely, he writes, "For you have been born again, not of perishable seed but of imperishable, through the living and enduring word of God." Thus, the Holy Spirit uses the Bible to give us the new birth by his divine power.

Then, in the next chapter (2:1–3), Peter draws his conclusion: "Therefore, rid yourselves of all malice and all deceit, hypocrisy, envy, and slander of every kind. Like newborn babies, crave pure spiritual milk, so that by it you may grow up in your salvation, now that you have tasted that the Lord is good." It's the Holy Spirit's work not only to give us the new birth, but also to enable that new nature that is like Jesus to grow in us to maturity. He uses God's Word, the Bible—preached, discussed, and read—to conform our thinking, feeling, and judgment more and more to be like Jesus' divine, perfect imitation of our heavenly Father.

Thus, Paul's call to be filled with the Spirit means that God gradually gives us an ever-increasing measure of his Spirit to restore us to the image and likeness of his divine nature. Adam and Eve's fall into the devil's deception—thinking they could rise to God's level and run their own lives—severely damaged their similarity to God.

Ephesians 5:18 also means that we must pray every day for the filling of the Holy Spirit, since the verb "be filled" in the original Greek has ongoing action in passive action. That is, only God can give us the Holy Spirit who operates independently from our feelings, but who also creates our spiritual improvement. However, we need to ask for his filling daily, because his work continues in us all the time.

I pray every day, and often many times throughout the day, that God will fill me with the Holy Spirit so that I can continue to have his spiritual gift of creativity through writing. I want to be God's agent of blessing in your life, dear reader.

Therefore, the joy that the Holy Spirit gives is much deeper and more permanent than the temporary human happiness of liquid spirits. What's more, the more we experience the Holy Spirit's running and improving our lives, the more we desire his influence through the Word of God. I've read the Bible from beginning to end many times, and God is more desirable each time I read his Word. I give credit to the Holy Spirit for making "the old, old story" ever new!

Bible Discussion Questions:
1. Read Psalm 104. What gifts has our Creator given to his human creatures? To believers? What is your response to him? Why?
2. Read Proverbs 20:1 and Ecclesiastes 2:1–3. What is true wisdom from God? What is secular life without God like, according to the author of Ecclesiastes? What is the futility of eating and drinking without focus on God as our Creator? What form does focus on God take in believers' lives concerning drinking alcohol?
3. In this connection, read Ephesians 5:18 in the context of the surrounding verses. How does Paul compare our spiritual growth to taking off and putting on clothes? How can we take off the old nature and put on the new nature more and more? What drinking activity does Paul forbid? How can we "be filled with the Spirit"? Explain by giving your personal experiences, always giving credit to God.
4. Which of the jokes included in this chapter hit home with you the most? Why?

* * *

One Step on Our Journey with Jesus: Resolve to pray fervent prayers of praise for your Creator's greatness every time you eat and drink anything. Pray daily for God to fill you with the Holy Spirit, so that he may make you more and more like Jesus Christ. If you have problems with impulsive eating or drinking anything, pray persistently for God, through Jesus' victory, to replace your impulsiveness with self-control. Tell other people whom God has put near you the victories that God gives you, always giving him the credit.

* * *

As we journey with Jesus toward perfection, we pause to discover his will about...

Chapter Four

PLAYING CARD, VIDEO, BOARD GAMES, AND THE LOTTERY; DANCING; MOVIEGOING

In this chapter, I group card playing, dancing, and moviegoing together because people in some traditions prohibited Christians' participation in those amusements during the 1900s. Why would people condemn such "innocent" pleasures? I will explore the answer to that question in this chapter, but first I will examine what God has to do with such fun.

What God says about playing cards

First of all, we have seen that our culture has secularized such kinds of fun by separating God from them, even in the minds of many Christians. They think that such pursuits as card playing and other games are a matter of "luck" or "chance." People say, "O, you were unlucky," when a person gets the wrong cards, dice, dominoes, or scrabble tiles.

Many of our spiritual ancestors saw the danger in card playing, because it was often associated with gambling. Our denomination warned against it back in the 1920s, and many people took that warning as a law against doing it at all, perhaps an unintended result. The same is true for dancing and moviegoing, which I will take up shortly.

However, the Bible's principles do not prohibit such fun, nor do they say that doing them in a secular way is correct. Here, we have to find the Bible's middle way.

Let's investigate what God has to do with such pleasures, if anything.

During our traveling adventure in pleasure, we go to Proverbs 16:33: "The lot is cast into the lap, but its every decision is from the LORD." This passage's teaching may be a shock to many Christians, but God's Word here flies in the face of secular attempts to distance God from games of "chance." As many Bible passages say, God guides his creation to engineer the course of events, even with pleasurable games. This passage clearly says that God guides the cards, dominoes, scrabble tiles, and dice, as well as Internet and video games that he gives you.

Another passage is Proverbs 16:9: "In his heart man plans his course, but the LORD determines his steps." Here, inspired Solomon teaches both human responsibility for all of our actions and God's plan that brings good out of losses in believers' lives.

Now, why does God sometimes give people wins and losses at other times? When our children were young, before smart phones, we played board games with them and intentionally chose not to let them win all of the time, because we all need to learn that we will not always win in life. I believe that God wants to teach us his lessons of humility when we win and patience when we lose games. Our children had a hard time losing and tended to gloat when they won.

However, God is involved in every fun event in some way. Meditate on Proverbs 16:33 and ask God to show you how he guides your fun and what lessons he means to teach you from them.

What about the lottery?

I personally don't "play" the lottery. My reasons follow:

(1) The odds against winning are huge. As far as I'm concerned, it's not a good investment because of those odds. A better use of those bucks is giving them to worthy causes through the church or in worthwhile organizations. I determine a worthy cause by asking for a statement of their beliefs and a recent audit of their finances. If the amount of their administrative overhead is more than 20 percent, I will not give to them.

(2) How many people play the lottery without any greed for a lot of money? Greed is unbiblical. Paul equated it with idolatry, and both Jesus and he condemned the selfish desire for more money, which is greed.

(3) My privacy would be ruined by such a win. People would always want me to "invest" in this or that scheme. Such a huge amount of money would create a lot of unwanted stress.

(4) I don't want to use God's money to invest in a microscopic chance of winning more.

(5) People have told me that the winnings go to a good cause, education. My response is that half of the money goes to the winners, while half goes to education. If you want to benefit education and if you feel that God wants you to, eliminate the middle person and send a check to your local school, rather than letting half of it go to winners, many of whom will blow it on selfish pleasure.

My point is that all of our money belongs to God, and we need to use it in a God-honoring way. For me, the lottery is just not one of those ways.

What God says about dancing

What does God say about dancing? On our terrific trip toward perfection, we investigate God's pleasure and ours in a psalm of praise to God, Psalm 149. "Praise the LORD! Sing to the LORD a new song, his praise in the assembly of the saints. Let Israel rejoice in their Maker; let the people of Zion be glad in their King. Let them praise his name with dancing and make music to him with tambourine and harp. For the LORD takes delight in his people; he crowns the humble with salvation. Let the saints rejoice in this honor and sing for joy on their beds" (verses 1–5).

Several observations about this passage are necessary:

(1) Notice that God feels pleasure when observing his faithful people and enjoys giving "the humble ... salvation."
(2) Then the psalmist calls us to reflect his joy in us back to him in joyful praising, singing, dancing, and making music—all focused on our Creator and Deliverer.
(3) Some people's prohibition of dancing in the 1920s and the following decades was a reaction to the immorality happening in dance halls then. When dancing happens in joyful praise to our great God of grace, God has fun, too, according to this inspired psalm.
(4) In many cultures, the pendulum swung from the church's reaction against our fun by legislating away secular pleasures to believers' conforming to our culture's separation of God from pleasure.
(5) This psalm guides us to the biblical middle way, that is, doing fun activities, including dancing, in praise to the God of creation who delivers us through Jesus.
(6) If we can find no way to praise God in our fun, we should abstain and find only activities during which we can center our pleasure on him.
(7) Of course, dancing done for selfish fun, romance, and lust is wrong. It all depends on our motives.

What God says about watching movies

However, God's involvement when we watch movies is less obvious, for the reason that no one had seen movies in the days of the Bible. Today, movies are available "on demand" on my TV remote for a prominent TV service. More of us watch movies on Netflix, cable, or satellite than go to the movie theater.

Then how can we discern what movies to watch and which ones to avoid? A principle from Romans 8:28 is helpful. If we choose to watch any movies, Paul writes, "And we know that in all things God works for the good of those who love him, who have been called according to his purpose." People have often applied this verse to unpleasant events in our lives, but its teaching also says, "If you play cards, dance, or watch movies, God works for your good in those actions too."

What good does God mean to bring about through movies?

First, if you can't find any good in movies, you shouldn't watch them.

Second, if you choose to watch them, God wants you to choose the ones through which his goodness and other qualities as your Creator and Rescuer can shine.

For example, I enjoy God through the science fiction *Star Wars* films. They portray weak good overcoming strong evil, especially in the first three movies that were made. When I watch those movies, God reminds me of the similar biblical theme—that he makes us weak people strong in his power through Jesus' mighty victory to overcome evil forces that attempt to undo us. Such is our need as we travel with Jesus, our Path and Guide, toward the future new universe. We need to seek his strength rather than follow him in our own power.

However, I also have to replace in my mind the *Star Wars'* "Force" with the Bible's 3-in-1 God, since the Force is the "spirit" of the universe and also the false, pantheistic god of the New Age, Hinduism, Buddhism, and traditional Native American beliefs. One main character in the original film explains that the Force is the sum total of all human spirits. In other words, pantheism believes that God is the same as the universe, not its Creator.

Other examples are the movies *Dances with Wolves* and *Amadeus*, both American Academy Award best pictures. The first film depicts a Northern Army officer during the Civil War, who decides to go west to the frontier Dakotas and who, after several contacts with the Lakota Sioux American Indians, becomes one of them and marries a white woman who also became a Sioux. Besides the beautiful music for which I praise God, the film gives me understanding and sympathy for a Native American culture. It also reminds me of the danger of blending in with any culture without examining it from a biblical point of view. Of course, one reason the film interests me is that my last church before I retired as a pastor was on the Lakota Sioux Rosebud Reservation in South Dakota, where I made some Lakota friends.

The other movie with the unusual title, *Amadeus*, is about the composer Mozart's relationships and amazing musical talent. Mozart was a hedonist who wrote spectacular classical music all day long and partied with his friends all night. His harmonious music was already fully finished in his head before he wrote it down. I marvel at God's gift of extraordinary musical talent in such a weak, spoiled person, showing God's greatness in human fallenness. To say the least, Mozart drank and partied himself to an early grave. Sadly, what did his pursuit of pleasure leave him? He gained nothing in this life, since it killed him.

The other main character in *Amadeus*—which, by the way, is Mozart's middle name meaning "loved of God"—is Antonio Salieri, who develops strong jealousy and hatred for Mozart's talent and for God, whom he feels gives him a desire to compose music without the corresponding musical gift. Of course, he gets it all wrong by making seven false assumptions about God. He ends up blaming himself for plotting Mozart's death.

One other movie is *The Ten Commandments,* with Charlton Heston as Moses. My mother took me to watch that film in 1958 when it was first shown in the movie theaters, the way she did to the other religious movies in the '50s. We had just begun attending a Baptist church, where I first heard the good news about Jesus' free acceptance of believers because of his life, death, and resurrection. *The Ten Commandments* showed me the opening of the Red Sea the way the Bible describes that amazing miracle. It enables the Israelites to escape the evil Pharaoh, king of the Egyptians, who has let them leave Egypt but then wants to bring them back. God impressed me with his unlimited power by using that movie and other means to bring me to true faith, though it adds unbiblical drama.

I share with you these examples to show you ways in which you can find value in a small minority of present-day films that are worthwhile. I find that I have to search through them like looking for a needle in a haystack to find the few that I can watch to honor God. However, such quality movies are out there.

Bible Discussion Questions:

1. Read Proverbs 16:9 and 33. What do these verses say about God's relationship with humans in their actions and fun? How do they disagree with the secular approach to life and pleasure? How can they change your approach to pleasurable activities? Explain by giving examples.
2. What do you think about the author's reasons for not playing the lottery? Do you agree or disagree with him? Give your reasons for your position.
3. Read Psalm 149:1–5 and re-read the author's comments. Which of his observations strike you as helpful for your Christian life, especially your fun? How can dancing be honoring to God? Explain.
4. Re-read 1 Corinthians 10:31 and Romans 8:28. How can you apply these passages to watching movies and having other kinds of fun? Explain.
5. What are your responses to the author's approach to fun in this chapter? Why?

* * *

One Step on Our Journey with Jesus: Take stock of your present uses of playing cards and other games, dancing, the lottery, or watching movies. Pray to God for his guidance in the ways he wants you to change your present patterns to fit them to his will. When he gives you a measure of insight about how you can have fun with praise and prayer in your mind, share that victory with people whom God has put near you.

* * *

- How is watching a movie different from reading a book?
- What we put into our minds eventually comes out of our mouth & we start accepting things we used to abhor?
- Expressions:
  What the hell.
  Don't give a damn? } unbecoming of
  Frigg because. Fuck } Christians,
  OMG,

While we limp lovingly with Jesus toward our final goal, let's examine...

Chapter Five

WATCHING TV AND SPORTS, READING BOOKS

God's pleasure in blessing his people

I turn to Psalm 103 to discover God's fun in showing his love. That psalm is filled with calls to praise our God, meaning that we are to give him all of the credit for everything, even in our use of TV, sports, and books.

The psalmist begins with the command of the writer to himself. "Praise the LORD, O my soul; all my inmost being, praise his holy name." By the way, you may know that the command "praise the LORD" translates the Hebrew word "hallelujah," which is one of the two words that are understood in most languages. The other word is "amen," which means "may it be so."

Anyway, the writer continues to list God's qualities for which we are to praise or honor him, especially his forgiving love. Then, in verses 13–18, he describes God's relationship or covenant with believers: "As a father has compassion on his children, so the LORD has compassion on those who fear him; for he knows how we are formed, he remembers that we are dust. As for man, his days are like grass, he flourishes like a flower of the field; the wind blows over it and it is gone, and its place remembers it no more. But from everlasting to everlasting the LORD's love is with those who fear him, and his righteousness with their children's children—with those who keep his covenant and remember to obey his precepts."

Several comments are necessary in response to this spiritually-rich psalm:

(1) The psalmist uses God's name "LORD" or Yahweh as his name that is associated with his personal relationship or covenant with all Old and New Testament true believers. It means "the eternally-faithful-to-his-promises God" revealed to Moses in the unburnable burning bush in Exodus chapters 3 and 4.

(2) The LORD's compassion is basically his sympathy in action toward his creatures and also all true believers as his children or God-fearers (see the book of Jonah for God's compassion for his creatures in contrast to Jonah's selective compassion).

(3) We are "dust," a reference to God's creation of Adam from dirt. Thus, the writer, at God's direction, puts us in our humble place.

(4) Our life is also "like grass" or short-lived, a meaningful reference in the dry land of Israel.

(5) In divine contrast to our temporary life, God's love for his own covenant people lasts forever, even to our grandchildren.

We need to pray for the fulfillment of this promise when our descendants go astray from God! We also need to be God's gentle, loving, gracious influence in their lives.

(6) The result of our true trust in the 3-in-1 God of the Scriptures is our faithful obedience to his will, which is revealed in the Bible, his covenant laws and "precepts."

The psalmist ends his amazing composition with renewed commands from God. "Praise the LORD, all his works everywhere in his dominion. Praise the LORD, O my soul." We are all God's works; therefore, this command is for us as well as for the inspired writer.

"Signs You're Watching Too Much TV" from jokes.com:

You need to be tranquilized when cable TV goes out.

In the late evening, you look forward to sitting back and catching the latest infomercial.

You try to impress the opposite sex by saying, "Hey, I get 120 channels!"

Your entire DVD collection consists of "Greatest TV Hits" albums by the decade.

You have a gold-plated channel-changer.

Your intellectual discussions all stem from The Discovery Channel.

After 15 minutes of work, you need a three-minute break.

The following comments from upwave.com describe some people's approach to TV:

"It's been a busy week, and now you're curled up on the couch alone—just you and your big bowl of reduced-fat kettle corn—watching your seventh episode of *The Golden Girls* in a row. Four hours later, do you say to yourself, "I feel great!" or "I wish I'd gone out with my friends instead"? Did the magic of television recharge your batteries, or did it enervate you? The answer might depend on your personality type.

"If your idea of a recharge is a few hours on the couch alone with Blanche and Dorothy, you might be an introvert. More to the point, being around other people may feel more like work than chill time for you, according to clinical psychologist Dr. Ramani Durvasula. She says introverts prefer to read, watch TV, take long walks or do other solo activities, and if they do choose to be around others, it's usually just a close friend or partner—not a group. '[Introverts] are not so chatty,' she says.

"Extroverts, on the other hand, often seem like 'people junkies,' says Durvasula. They find social gatherings or places with lots of people and activities relaxing, and love meeting new people or cultivating old relationships. Extroverts don't have to be in noisy settings in order to relax, but they're more likely to want to chill out with other people. The noisy party that feels like work for an introvert might be the antidote to stress for an extrovert, according to Durvasula."

Furthermore, psychology.com states, "Extroversion is a core factor of personality and is difficult to modify. But generally speaking, the only people bothered by extroverts' volubility and drive are the introverted members of their circle!"

I will share more about fun events later in this book, but I guess that I was an introvert when I was a child and teenager, but God added some extrovert to my personality when I was a sales manager and then a pastor.

At any rate, whether you are an introvert or extrovert, your choices of entertainment without God and only for selfish pleasure produce empty, temporary fun. Furthermore, God can change our personalities to be more God-honoring, regardless of our makeup.

Human watching of TV in the light of God's will

Most of us watch TV but are often reluctant to admit to it. As I said earlier in this book (chapter 1), before I became a Christ-follower, I was hooked on TV and sports as a child and into adulthood. It was a mental escape from the farm. I carried that idol with me for several years after I became a Christian and then a pastor. Many people use those activities and/or books to gain temporary relief from the stresses and boredom of life, as I did, just the way many people use the other pleasures described in this book to run away from life's harsh reality.

I also shared with you God's rescue from my escapism expressed in my "sports-and-TV-aholism" so that I now praise him for the TV programs and sports events that I watch.

However, even though God's Word says nothing directly about TV, the Bible does give God's estimate of human puffed-up pride that TV often shows: "Whom did the LORD consult to enlighten him, and who taught him the right way? Who was it that taught him knowledge or showed him the path of understanding? Surely the nations are like a drop in a bucket; they are regarded as dust on the scales; he weighs the islands as though they were fine dust" (Isaiah 40:14–5). The God of the Bible is our Creator; we are not his creators but merely his human creatures.

One of those "precepts" to which I return again is 1 Corinthians 10:31: "So whether you eat or drink or whatever you do, do it all for the glory of God." I had to admit that I was not following this verse at all in my TV and sports watching, and I'm sure that few Christians in any fun-loving culture have reflected at all on how God relates to their entertainment, including TV watching. People often use TV and sports as their temporary escape from the emptiness of life, as I did from farm drudgery.

God, through Paul, is laying down his universal rule, though, for all fun activities, but I will apply it to our pleasure.

For example, what TV and sports can we watch to honor God? We can all answer that question differently, but the following ways are how God led me to choose certain programs as my way to honor God and to avoid others.

For my TV watching, the main idea or premise of a program is very important. To give you an example, my praising God for American TV "justice" dramas like *NCIS, CSI, Blue Bloods, Elementary, Hawaii 5-0*, and other ones starts with their overall purpose. I call them "justice" rather than "crime" dramas, because the overall purpose of all those shows is to catch criminals and provide justice on behalf of their victims. If the criminals start winning those battles, I will find other programs to watch. In my way of thinking, such programs show God's justice in pursuing and punishing evil and sin in his world through the police or forensic people.

Moreover, when the main characters are a man and a woman, I enjoy their professional interactions and reasoning process in finding and building a case against the bad guys. However, when their relationship becomes sexual outside of marriage, it spoils the show for me and I tune out, as I did with *Bones*.

When I look at "unreality" shows, which I have watched at other people's houses, I find their premises or main ideas undesirable. On the long-running *Survivor* program, someone is voted off the program every week, which reflects, to me, the sinful human idea that we need to measure up in other people's and in God's eyes in order to be acceptable. That kind of overall view in a TV series turns me off, so that I have sworn off watching all "unreality" shows.

Instead, I prefer fictional programs, because I can distance my mind from them. After all, if someone is killed in that kind of show, I know that the actor will "rise from the dead" after the cameras stop filming and the director yells "cut." Thus, I can detach myself from it and think about how it relates to God much more than shows in which people fall in water trying to win some money or sing for some grand prize.

Now, these comments are my own reactions to different kinds of TV programing to illustrate how anyone can apply biblical truth to television. If you can find ways to praise the Lord for what you watch, and those shows are different from mine, that kind of approach is good for you. However, I do find that I have to sift through many TV programs to find ones worth watching. Therefore, I prefer to have a TV service that gives me many channels.

Another Bible passage is Proverbs 21:16–17, which is a chilling reminder of God's direction to give all of our pleasure to him and applies this topic to all of the forms of pleasure in this book. "A man who strays from the path of understanding comes to rest in the company of the dead. He who loves pleasure will become poor; whoever loves wine and oil will never be rich." In interpreting these verses, we must remember that the wisdom literature of Psalms and Proverbs makes general observations about life to which there are exceptions, as the writers apply God's will to readers' lives.

Thus, Solomon warns us that failing to relate any experiences to God and, as a result, living only for ourselves in selfish pleasure leads to grave consequences. Jesus describes the result of leaving God out of our lives as eventually dying and going into "outer darkness" in hell. Another description of that disastrous place is a lake with burning sulfur in the book of Revelation chapter 20.

I hope that you, dear reader, will not experience that terrible result. Instead, we need to trust in Jesus' life, death, and resurrection as our ticket to this life's journey on our path to God and to his final resting place in the next life.

Moreover, not everyone in this life will become poor because they love pleasure, as Solomon says, but they will be extremely poverty-striken in the next life if they rely on their selfish pleasure to give them "happiness," thus, living only for their hedonistic fun. Of course, many true stories demonstrate that some people who win the lottery become poor again because of their misuse of God's blessing of wealth.

Bible Discussion Questions:
1. Read Psalm 103. What parts of that hymn or psalm of praise are the hardest for Christians to fulfill in terms of their fun life? For what parts do you praise the LORD? Explain.
2. Read 1 Corinthians 10:31 with the paragraph around it. How can you apply this text to your TV watching? In other words, what programs can you watch to honor God, and which ones would you avoid because you can't honor God when you watch them? What do you think about the author's approach to TV watching? Explain your reaction.
3. Read Proverbs 21:16–17. In what ways does unrepentant love of pleasure (hedonism) bring poverty in this life? In the next life? Why?

* * *

One Step on Our Journey with Jesus: With prayer for God's guidance, pick the TV programs with which you can genuinely praise God for his creative or rescuing power. Then decide to avoid those that distract you from focusing on God. As always, balance your watching with other priorities to which God has called you.

* * *

God's gift of believers' pleasure in him as our Creator

Now that God has put us in our insignificant place as his creatures *much, much* smaller than he is, we need to examine what ways we can use TV to lift him up as our all-powerful Maker. We need to look at Philippians 4:8–9 for God's guidance through Paul: "Finally, brothers, whatever is true, whatever is noble, whatever is pure, whatever is lovely, whatever is admirable—if anything is excellent or praiseworthy—think about such things. Whatever you have learned or received or heard from me, or seen in me—put into practice. And the God of peace will be with you."

In this passage, Paul uses words from the unbelieving culture around him to describe the content of the world's best. Why does Paul command us to think about secular parts of our culture?

The reason is that he believes that God, as the infallible Creator of the earth and its inhabitants, reveals himself through fallible people and his fallen creation (Romans 1:18–20). The problem is that, as the Romans passage says, humans substitute the things and people of his creation for him as their Source.

Personal examples of praise for God with sports

For example, for the first thirty years of my life, I *enjoyed myself* instead of God with my use of TV and sports and, before that time, radio. However, God broke through to me by convicting me of my selfish pleasure and teaching me to praise him for what I view on TV (see chapter 1).

As a result, in sports, I used to watch wrestling and boxing when I was younger. I no longer watch them, because wrestling is a fake show with glorified stunt men and women. An ex-professional wrestler's speech gave me that knowledge when I was a new Christian.

In addition, a member of one of my churches said that he watched boxing for 10 percent of the action that was truly self-defense. I responded that I couldn't watch a sport in which I can only praise God 10 percent of the time.

Moreover, a good friend of mine enjoys attending drag-racing events. He says that he has met many drag racing people and has had many chances to witness to them. However, my opinion is that I can't enjoy a sport that expects us to be excited about a very short amount of action like a horse or drag race.

Furthermore, I prefer to praise God for sports that involve his gift of human talent unassisted by cars and horses. As a result, the ones for which God has enabled me to praise him with the deepest, longest lasting, and most spiritual satisfaction are baseball, basketball, football, tennis, golf, and the Olympics. All of them are sports that I have tried to do in one way or another. (I swim, and when the Olympics add an over-seventy, backstroke event, I'll enter it.) Because I've tried those sports in some fashion, I can appreciate the special, amazing athletic skills that God has given those athletes. They make their sports look easy, while, in reality, they are very difficult.

Now, you don't have to like any of those sports through which I enjoy God as those athletes' Creator. Someone might say to me, "How can you enjoy some of those sports when those sports stars are so greedy?"

I respond, "Yes, all of those people are sinners just like me. I praise the Lord for revealing his creative power in their great abilities and let God judge their weaknesses, because I'm weak, too."

In watching American baseball, I enjoy God's gifts of the hitters' great hand-eye coordination and the pitchers' abilities to change speeds, rotations, and locations of their pitches over the seventeen-inch plate to keep batters off-balance. I also enjoy the duals between pitchers and hitters, revealing to me the best of God's creative power. In all of the places that we have lived, I have also added many favorite teams.

When I watch American basketball, I praise the Creator for the players' agility, speed, endurance, and teamwork, as well as the coaches' ingenuity in devising ways to overcome the other teams' defenses and offenses. The same observation holds true for football coaches' outstanding abilities to counteract the other coaches' strategies.

With American football, I appreciate God's amazing power to enable wide receivers to catch passes with acrobatic skill and quarterbacks to pass exactly where they need to complete their passes. I also marvel at God's gift of coaching ingenuity to call the right play to overcome the other teams' defenses.

In all of the team sports in the Olympics, I praise God for the players' abilities to work together to accomplish their goals. In the individual sports of tennis, golf, and the Olympics, I'm in awe of the amazing talents on display in God's creation.

For example, I failed archery class in college physical education with the easiest P.E. professor. I couldn't hit the target with the arrow, no matter how hard I tried. As a result, I had to find another sport to take. I chose tennis, in which I could at least get the ball over the net. I guess the reason is that the "target" was a bit larger than the one in archery. To this day, I enjoy God's gifts of endurance, quickness, power, and speed of players' bodies as they somehow skim the ball over the net consistently and with great velocity.

I also enjoy good golfers' amazing coordination to be able to send the golf ball where they want it to go. When I golfed as a duffer rather than a golfer, I couldn't control that little round sphere nearly as well. Thus, I can greatly appreciate God in his blessing on the professional golfers' use of their athletic bodies.

During the 2014 World Cup of soccer or football, I tried to get interested in that sport, but without success, because many games have little or no scoring.

To me, all of the sports and teams that I follow represent the best of God's creation, according to Philippians 4:8–9, for which I give him all of the honor by his powerful grace.

Enjoying God in the world of books

When we look at the world of books, we find that the technological age threatens to distract people from reading books. What can we gain from reading books and e-books?

When I was an English teacher in Christian schools, I tried to teach the students to be Christian literary critics, comparing and contrasting the values and experiences of literary writers and characters to the Bible's truths. Later, when I became a pastor/

preacher/teacher in seven churches, I shared the ways in which the church members could apply God's Word to their everyday experiences and to find Jesus' progressive victory. Now, as a writer of Christian books, my ministry is not much different, since God is using me to help you, my dear reader, apply the Bible to your life for your spiritual advancement.

While I was a preacher, however, I had little time to read for either information or enjoyment beyond my Bible study for two Sunday messages every week. Frankly, after spending all day in enjoyable study to prepare those sermons, I had little desire to be involved with more books in the evening, even for pleasure.

When God gave me a retirement writing ministry, I started reading in order to improve my writing. For example, I've read several novels in order to prepare to write my first novel, which God has enabled me to begin writing. Several novelists have shown me how to write their kind of fiction as I read their books. Thus, reading has become a means to the end of writing improvement for God's praise.

Since I have never read books just for pleasure, you will have to take the passages and ideas of this book and apply them yourself to your pleasurable reading. However, as you read, I hope that you can find God's grace to "rejoice in the Lord always."

Bible Discussion Questions:

1. Read Philippians 4:8–9. What is Paul's point about our thought life? Why?

Pray and Play

2. Go back to Philippians 4:4. For whom should we experience our fun—ourselves, other people, or God? Why? How can we rejoice in our God with our pleasurable activities? Explain.
3. For which of the sports that the author watches can you praise God? For what sports can you honestly honor the Creator? Or do you avoid all sports? Give your reasons for each answer.
4. What is your favorite approach to the world's TV, sports, and books—separatism (separating from them), modernism (blending in with them without thinking about God), or Paul's approach of finding the best of God's creation with which to "rejoice in the Lord always"? Explain your reasoning.

* * *

One Step on Our Journey with Jesus: Think about the kinds of pleasurable events—sports or otherwise—with which you can praise and meditate on your great Creator, and begin to use your mind to focus on him during those events or performances. As he gives you the ability to praise him during your fun, tell someone about God's change in your life.

* * *

As we labor on Jesus' path, moving toward our final destination, let's consider...

Chapter Six

WORK AND VOLUNTEERING

Motivations to work or volunteer

Consider the following humorous description from greatcleanjokes.com a few years ago:

I've been tired for some time. For a couple of years I've been blaming it on lack of sleep and too much pressure from my job, but now I found out the real reason: I'm tired because I'm overworked.

The population of this country is 237 million. 104 million are retired. That leaves 133 million to do the work.

There are 85 million in school, which leaves 48 million to do the work.

Of this there are 29 million employed by the federal government, leaving 19 million to do the work.

2.8 million are in the Armed Forces, which leaves 16.2 million to do the work.

Take from the total the 14,800,000 people who work for State and City Governments and that leaves 1.4 million to do the work.

At any given time there are 188,000 people in hospitals, leaving 1,212,000 to do the work.

Now, there are 1,211,998 people in prisons.

That leaves just two people to do the work. You and me.

And you're sitting at your computer reading jokes!

This joke makes deliberate exaggeration to make the point that we can get overworked with all the demands that our jobs put on us.

Why do we work so hard? Why do we volunteer to do worthwhile activities to help others? Often, people work for money with which to accomplish their goals in life. Also, people volunteer their time to feel better about themselves or to get an emotional high or to get other people's admiration. These motives and others are often self-centered, not God-centered, and often remain unexamined.

God uses the prophet Hosea to criticize Israel's external religion and their rebellion against examining their inner life and motivations: "What can I do with you, Ephraim [the northern kingdom]? What can I do with you, Judah [the southern kingdom]? Your love is like the morning mist, like the early dew that disappears. Therefore I cut you in pieces with my prophets; I killed you with the words of my mouth; my judgments flashed like lightning upon you. For I desire mercy, not sacrifice, and acknowledgment of God rather than burnt offerings. Like Adam, they have broken the covenant—they were unfaithful to me there" (Hosea 6:4–7). Similarly, professing Christians today spend a little time praying before meals and attending a worship service on Sunday, but they use precious few days reading God's Word and reflecting on

God's will that calls them to devoting all of their time, including work and volunteering, to God through Jesus.

In fact, a large number of people use work or volunteering as pleasure. However, if they don't commit it to God, it's like the Israelites' love—a morning mist that disappears quickly as the day goes on.

Rather, God's pleasure is in our work and volunteering when we give those activities to him daily to be used as worthwhile activities in his creation.

For example, in my first job, when I worked in a USA Illinois Tollway restaurant as a short-order cook the summer before I attended college for my first year, I shared with other employees my feeling that God wanted me to be a minister. Then one day, the German-born manager marched up to me and said, "I hear that you want to be a priest."

I replied, "Yes, I feel that God wants me to be a minister in the church."

He stiffly said, "Then you can have Sundays off!" and stalked away. I was thankful for God's blessing of Sundays off to worship with God's people, since that restaurant never closed.

However, many people live their work lives waiting for the weekend when they can engage in pleasure. In other words, for them, work is only a means for attaining fun during the rest of their time.

In any case, self-centeredness reigns in many people's work and volunteering lives. However, we've already seen that God isn't pleased with mere outward obedience in any area of our lives. Rather, he sees our hearts' motivations and wants us to give our daily lives to him in work and volunteering.

Godly motivation to work and volunteer resulting in God's pleasure

After the writer to the Hebrews describes Jesus' death as our divine high priest substituting himself for us in his death, God inspires him to declare, "Through Jesus, therefore, let us continually offer to God a sacrifice of praise—the fruit of lips that confess his name. And do not forget to do good and to share with others, for with such sacrifices God is pleased" (Hebrews 13:15–16). Notice that God calls us to give our lives as constant "sacrifices" of praise. The word "sacrifice" refers to the Old Testament slaughtered animals that people bring to the place of worship to die in their place. Such sacrifices look forward to Jesus' one suffering sacrifice on the cross to declare us "not guilty" and right with him as our Judge.

Similarly, God calls us to be living sacrifices in Romans 12:1–2: "Therefore, I urge you, brothers, in view of God's mercy, to offer your bodies as living sacrifices, holy and pleasing to God—this is your spiritual act of worship. Do not conform any longer to the pattern of this world, but be transformed by the renewing of your mind. Then you will be able to test and approve what God's will is—his good, pleasing, and perfect will."

These two passages yield several observations for our work and volunteering lives:

(1) Notice that in both passages, our surrender to God's will for our lives is "pleasing" to him.

(2) Therefore, God feels pleasure when we give our work and volunteer lives to him as our worship, which is not to be reserved only for the day of group worship. Work is worship, either of ourselves or of God.

(3) Notice that the writer to the Hebrews says that our sacrifice or surrender involves doing good and sharing with others, far from selfish actions.

(4) The Romans passage begins practical verses that apply God's "mercy" or grace that covers our guilty situation before him through Jesus' death. Thus, our loving surrender of our lives, including our work, flows out of Jesus' rescue from God's just anger at our selfish rebellion (chapters 1–11).

(5) God the Father can only be pleased with us because of his perfect pleasure with Jesus' perfect pleasure in going to the Roman death instrument in our place.

(6) Therefore, it is only through our response in faith to God's free pleasure at Jesus' ultimate self-surrender that he accepts us freely.

(7) Notice that Paul calls us to our lives as "holy and pleasing" sacrifices to God. Of course, "holy" means "separated" for God to use us in our work and volunteering.

Personal work experiences

God has given me a great variety of work and volunteering activities to do during summers while I was teaching and while he was preparing me to enter seminary to be a pastor. I've worked in seven different factories from two hours to ten weeks. I've worked in landscaping and as a restaurant cook. God has also led me to collect garbage, lay concrete, and make manholes.

For example, one summer, I learned how to lay sod for a landscaping company, before they put me on a landscaping job with a boss who didn't believe in breaks even though the job was very heavy labor. We had only a few minutes to wolf down our lunches. God had sent rain, and the boss backed a dump truck full of black dirt under the house's overhang and got it stuck in the mud. However, he couldn't elevate the back of the truck to empty the dirt.

Therefore, we laborers had to shovel it out of the truck by hand, but he wouldn't even allow us to rest after our backbreaking labor because his reckless actions got us behind schedule. Needless to say, that day was my last landscaping experience. With that boss, work was all dollar signs.

The next day, I put on my suit and applied at a boat factory. The guy who hired me already had a stack of applications but said that I was a good candidate for a shipping dock position. Thus, because God opened a boat-door, I joined the shipping crew loading boats on trucks. My shipping-dock boss was as nice a boss as the landscaper had been an insensitive dictator.

However, after three weeks, the factory's boat shipments stopped because of the "minor" matter in which the boats' hulls started cracking in half! I don't think that defect was my fault! For three more weeks, my kindly boss kept me on doing office work until he finally came up to me one day with a big frown on his face and said,

"I'm sorry, Bruce, but I have to let you go." Then I went to get my old job back at the Illinois Tollway restaurant.

What varied work experiences God gave me in that one summer during college! On the other hand, I didn't reflect in my younger days about how God related to my work; I just knew that I had to make money to go to college. During the early 1960s, we could actually work our way through college with God's blessing!

During college, I washed dishes, peeled potatoes, and "ran" the food lines in the cafeteria, beginning with the salary of eighty cents an hour. Then, in my last two years, God provided a whopping salary of $1.25 an hour when he enabled me to become the evening snack shop manager on campus. I was really rolling in money then!

God also provided me with my first sales job as a Fuller Brush man, going door to door selling brushes and other products, when I studied to get my English master's degree. During my second teaching job, this time at a Christian high school, God led me to continue my Fuller Brush selling on the south side of Chicago and also to collect garbage one summer. I still didn't reflect on the connection between my work life and God during those summer jobs. Instead, I was working to pay fall insurance bills.

When I think back to those varied work experiences, I believe that God definitely provided those open doors to supply our family's growing needs. It's a shame that my motivation wasn't more God-centered.

Biblical reasons to work

However, after God renewed his call for me to be a pastor, I'm thankful that he gave me insight about godly work, even if it involves digging black dirt out of a stuck dump truck or lifting heavy garbage cans to empty them into a garbage truck as we clean up. We can provide a useful service or improve God's fallen creation in some way and praise him as a result.

Several Bible passages call us to work well. One verse is Ephesians 4:28: "He who has been stealing must steal no longer, but must work, doing something useful with his own hands, that he must have something to share with those in need." First, we notice two believing motives for work—producing God-honoring, useful results and sharing our income with needy people. How often do you think people have these motives for working hard? I believe that it's seldom.

Second, if we waste time on the job, we're stealing from our employer and from God. After all, "our" time is actually God's time. He calls us through Paul to stop such stealing.

Third, I believe that God has motivated me, based on his Word, to use all income from my writing ministry with which he blesses me to give half for the gospel's spread and use half for the expenses of publishing more books. After all, he has blessed me with a pension and U.S. Social Security to take care of our needs, both of which are delayed salary from thirty-eight years of productive work.

Another Bible passage is 1 Thessalonians 4:11–12, just before the verses describing Jesus' Second Coming: "Make it your ambition to lead a quiet life, to mind your own business, and to work with your own hands, just as we told you, so that your daily life may win the respect of outsiders and so that you will not be dependent on anybody."

Apparently, some of the Thessalonian believers have left their jobs in order to wait for Jesus' coming. Paul corrects their actions by writing these words to motivate them to work, so that unbelievers will respect them and God will support them through their work. If we're slacking off on our jobs that we no longer like, no one is going to respect our Christian witness to what God has done in our lives.

Therefore, God's Word, the Bible, is clear in calling us to work hard for God's honor in order to bless others, whether or not we get paid for it.

Bible Discussion Questions:

1. Read Hosea 6:4–7 with the whole chapter in mind. What does Hosea's preaching have to do with our work or volunteering life? Explain by giving examples from daily life.
2. Read Hebrews 13:15–16 and Romans 12:1–2. What do the writers mean when they call us to be sacrifices? How can we become such sacrifices? Give a practical example from life.
3. Read Ephesians 4:28 in the chapter's context. How does Paul contrast the self-centered ways of human activity and God's commands to live God-centered lives? In which verses in that chapter does Paul compare our need to take off the old nature and put on God's gift of the new nature with taking off old and putting on new clothes? Explain.

4. Read 1 Thessalonians 4:11–12. What other motives for working hard does God, through Paul, give us? Why don't Christians often have such unselfish incentives to work for God? How can God help us change to do godly work and volunteering? How can we experience Jesus' joy in our jobs? Explain with examples from your life.

* * *

One Step on Our Journey with Jesus: Add to your prayers the request to dedicate your productive activity completely to God, whether it's housework, volunteering, an occupation, or retirement. God will then make it pleasurable in a more satisfying way. Find an unbeliever near you at work or in your neighborhood, become that person's friend without adopting his or her lifestyle, and witness to that person about God's work in your life, leaving to God their future.

* * *

While we skip joyfully along Jesus' limited-access highway to our final goal, let's examine...

Chapter Seven

SEX

Human and biblical views about sexual activity

Any book about fun has to include a chapter about sex, or so it seems to me. Many Christians throughout the last two thousand years have adopted the idea that sex is a necessary evil and only for producing offspring, and that any other use of sexual actions is sinful. Others have developed the modern cavalier attitude that says, "As long as we're both consenting adults and no one gets hurt, having casual sex is okay." These two positions are both contrary to the Bible, God's Word, given to us for our good.

However, let's first look at God's pleasure about creating us as sexual beings. In Genesis 1:27, 31a, inspired Moses writes, after he describes human creatures' creation in God's likeness to be his assistant rulers over the earth, "So God created man in his own image, in the image of God he created him, male and female he created them....God saw all that he had made, and it was very good." Now, why do I refer to this text? Notice that God creates humans as perfect males and females. He makes sexual differences ("male and female") before humans botch their assignment to rule the world under their all-powerful Creator.

Thus, sex is good in the beginning but falls into self-centered use as the first pair rebels against their divine Benefactor. As a result, Jesus comes from the Father to rescue our use of sex.

The modern media is filled with "casual sex" and "free love." The Bible says otherwise. For example, in Genesis 38, Moses describes in some detail Judah's invitation to Tamar, his daughter-in-law, after her two husbands die and Judah sins with his affair with a prostitute who turns out to be Tamar in disguise. Moses contrasts such loose sexual morals on the part of the eventual head of one of the tribes of Israel—the one from which Jesus would come—with the following chapter (39), in which Joseph, an eventual patriarch of two tribes, becomes a slave in Egypt and rebuffs the seduction of Potiphar's wife to go to bed with her by running away from her.

The Bible, as God's revelation of his will, clearly calls us to keep our sexual desires and actions within marriage. The seventh commandment is, "You shall not commit adultery (Exodus 20:14)." However, Jesus extends it in his Sermon on the Mount: "You have heard that it was said, 'Do not commit adultery,' But I tell you that anyone who looks at a woman lustfully has already committed adultery with her in his heart" (Matthew 5:27–28).

A number of people have charged that the early church changed the New Testament according to their own ideas. However, making the seventh commandment much harder than the original commandment could not have happened if the early Christians altered it. In fact, people would never have included much of the Bible if they changed it. Examples are King David as an adulterer and murderer and Peter's three denials of knowing Jesus. As a result, that charge makes no sense. This difficult passage along with the whole Bible has to be Jesus' and the writers' original teaching, because no human would have written a harder command about sexual desire than the seventh commandment and many other passages.

Single Paul's teachings about sex

The Bible's definition of adultery is sex outside of marriage. The King James Bible translates the other term for sexual straying by single people "fornication." The NIV translates that same word "sexual immorality." For example, Paul deals with the Corinthians' continued performance of the loose sexual activity of their Greek culture as follows in 1 Corinthians 6:13b–20: "The body is not meant for sexual immorality, but for the Lord, and the Lord for the body. By his power God raised the Lord from the dead, and he will raise us also. Do you not know that your bodies are members of Christ himself? Shall I then take the members of Christ and unite them with a prostitute? Never! Do you not know that he who unites himself with a prostitute is one with her in body? For it is said, 'The two will become one flesh.' But he who unites himself with the Lord is one with him in spirit. Flee from sexual immorality. All other sins a man commits are outside his body, but he who sins sexually sins against his own body. Do you not know that your body is a temple of the Holy Spirit, who is in you, whom you have received from God? You are not your own; you were bought at a price. Therefore honor God with your body."

Note the following observations about Paul's comments on the topic of sex:

(1) The word translated "sexual immorality" in any New Testament context means sexual activity with anyone else by single people, whereas "adultery" means sex outside of marriage by married people.

(2) As believers in Jesus, our Deliverer and Boss, we belong to him (verse 13b—"the Lord"), and the Holy Spirit lives in us as his temple (verse 19). Therefore, honoring him with our bodies becomes necessary, no matter what values movies and TV try to teach us.

(3) If we are true believers, God, who resurrected Jesus, will raise our bodies also in addition to giving us resurrected life now through the miracle of the new birth. Therefore, our bodies are parts of Jesus' resurrected body. It would be treason to join ours with that of a nonspouse, because we are already part of his body.

(4) God's teaching here through Paul comes from Genesis 2:24. After God creates Eve from Adam's body, Moses gives God's inspired observation. "For this reason a man will leave his father and mother and be united to his wife, and they will become one flesh."

(5) Therefore, any sexual desire or action outside of the marriage commitment violates God's perfect will.
(6) Sexual sinning against our marriage partner is against God, who joins us to our spouse and to him.
(7) Draw your own conclusion about the ideas promoting homosexual marriage, which is physically impossible, because sexual intercourse is the external symbol of the marriage bond between a man and a woman.

For example, in connection with the TV "comedy" *Two and a Half Men*, the teenage star who has grown up on the popular American show became a Christian recently. At a press conference, he said that no one should watch his program, because it is a sleazy show with immoral values. I watched that program about two single dads raising a son of one of them. I lasted only about ten minutes before I found a better American TV show. Sad to say, that "comedy" about sexual immorality is still on TV at this time and will be in reruns for a long time. The fact that the American public watches it is a sad commentary on their values.

Furthermore, Paul writes another passage describing present-day sexual looseness almost 2,000 years ago (Romans 1:26–27). Once the human race in Adam and Eve replaces the Creator with the creation in their worship and daily lives, "…God gave them over to shameful lusts. Even their women exchanged natural relations for unnatural ones. In the same way the men also abandoned natural relations with women and were inflamed with lust for one another.

Men committed indecent acts with other men and received in themselves the due penalty for their perversion."

People have charged that such a description of human behavior is unclear, but it's only "unclear" if it contradicts human thinking and acting apart from God's gracious guidelines. Thus, homosexual and heterosexual conduct and desires outside of a public, lifelong, marital commitment of one man and one woman clearly violates God's will in his Word, the Bible.

Of course, God the Creator loves all people, gay and straight, whom we encounter, and we are to love them, too, while recognizing and avoiding their sins. It's through God's unconditional love shown by our accepting attitudes and actions toward them that he can draw unbelievers to himself and bring about repentance in their lives.

A personal example

For example, I share with my fictional friend Joe Smith in *Doubtbusters! God Is My Shrink!* my lust for women in my earlier years. Even though I was a Christian, I justified those desires because, after all, I hadn't committed the outward act of adultery. Well, God used the Matthew 5:27–28 passage, to which I have already referred, to convict me of my mental adultery. He also taught me that when I saw a beautiful woman, I began praising God for his amazing creative power in making the human body so beautiful. Jesus' victory made that change possible.

However, my lust for women was just as much sin as the actions of practicing homosexuals' lifestyles. God can enable, through Jesus' deliverance, all believers to overcome their desires and actions that stray outside of his will. We need to claim persistently Jesus' victory to control our thoughts, desires, and actions.

Sexual fun

On the other hand, sex within marriage, when it's God-honoring, can have the by-product of great pleasure. After all, when Paul writes Timothy about rich people's actions in the use of their wealth, he says that God gives us "everything for our enjoyment" (1 Timothy 6:17b). Paul's command elsewhere, of course, is to "rejoice in the Lord always" (Philippians 4:4). Therefore, the pleasure of believers' sex, as with all fun, must be centered on God, the Creator of our pleasure.

Bible Discussion Questions:

1. Read Genesis 1:26–31. What does this passage say about God's creation of human sexuality? How do you feel about the fact that God made us male and female? Explain.
2. Read Genesis 38 and 39 as well as Exodus 20:14. How does Moses contrast the sexual "adventures" of Judah and Joseph? What conclusions for your life would you make about sex outside of marriage along with God's commandment about it? Why?
3. Read Matthew 5:27–28. Why do you suppose that Jesus extends the meaning of the seventh commandment to inner desires? How can we obey Jesus' will? Explain.

4. Read 1 Corinthians 6:12–20 and Romans 1:18–27. What is God's opinion about sexual activity outside of marriage, even between "consenting adults"? Explain.
5. What point does the author make about 1 Timothy 6:17b, Philippians 4:4, and sex? How do you feel about his conclusion? Explain.

* * *

One Step on Our Journey with Jesus: Examine your own desires and actions to see if you are guilty of sexual sins. If so, confess them and persistently seek God's great grace to overcome them through Jesus' triumph by the Holy Spirit's power. When he gives you victory, share his change in your life with a close, trusted friend.

* * *

As we walk on the heavenly highway,
we examine the fun of...

Chapter Eight

ATTENDING PROFESSIONAL AND OTHER SPORTS EVENTS

God's creative power displayed in his creation

What can we say about our attendance at sports events? In Genesis 2:7, inspired Moses writes, "The LORD God formed man from the dust of the ground and breathed into his nostrils the breath of life, and the man became a living being." Here we see that the LORD—Yahweh, his name in relationship or covenant with humans—forms Adam's body and life. In sports events, those athletic skills that God gave to some people are on full display to our Creator's credit. Thus, why not give him honor for his creative power as we view such amazing talents, since he is their Source?

Moreover, the psalmist David says in Psalm 139 that God's divine nature is present everywhere (verses 1–12), and then gives the reason that he can't run away from God, the way Jonah tries to do. "For you created my inmost being; you knit me together in my mother's womb. I praise you because I am fearfully and wonderfully made; your works are wonderful, I know that full well" (verses 13–14). Notice that God creates us from conception and that David's response is to praise the LORD for his awesome power. Such reactions should be our responses to sports events that we attend and/or watch.

For example, hockey players, as well as all athletes at the Winter Olympics, reveal God the Maker's skill in creating those bodies that can move so well on ice or snow. I have attended one professional hockey game in my whole life. When we lived near Chicago, my landlord gave me and my friend free tickets to a Black Hawks' game. They won 10-4 in an amazing display of human talent. However, the crowd yelled louder for the three fights than for all of the goals combined. As a result, the crowd's bloodthirstiness turned me off to professional hockey's tolerance for violence. However, my friend enjoyed the fights the most.

My dislike for that sport continued even while we lived five years in Canada, where hockey is a very important part of the culture.

On the other hand, I have attended many other professional sports events—basketball and baseball games. I have watched innumerable other games on TV. Now, the only way I watch pro athletes is on TV.

Some people have said that they won't watch pro sports because of the athlete's high salaries. The way I see it, the charge is true that many sports stars are greedy and that money drives the sports industry.

However, all people in public life are sinners driven by selfishness, unless they are Christians. As with any public personalities, they will answer to the divine Judge for their imperfect motives.

By contrast, if I watch any sports, my responsibility before God is to acknowledge his great creative power in his gift of great athletic skills as I watch them play their sports. Then I let God judge them for their motivation.

In addition, I can no longer justify buying tickets because of the extremely high prices needed to pay the players' high salaries. The last time that I bought Chicago Cubs baseball tickets, at the end of the process, they slapped a $30 service fee on me. I e-mailed them that I would no longer purchase tickets from them, because they did not inform me upfront about the total cost. However, maybe my e-mail made a difference, since lately their ticket agency advertises that the upfront ticket price is the one you pay. That decision is too late for me.

Good news about two baseball players and a golfer

In contrast to the recent negative publicity about American athletes' performance-enhancing drug-taking and other sordid stories came a *Grand Rapids Press* news article by Associated Press' Jim Fitzgerald. The headline read "Baseball star rescues, renovates church." It turns out that the newly-retired, record-shattering New York Yankee pitcher, Mariano Rivera, who has the record for saving the most baseball games ever, has "for years credited God for his skills on the field." His foundation is now giving three million dollars to restore an old, crumbling, New Rochelle, New York, church, where his wife will continue her Christian ministry to other Christians and to the neighborhood.

Interestingly, I also came across an Internet item entitled "Play and Pray." It describes a professional baseball player and his wife. He plays the games, while his wife prays for him. It's good that they rely on prayer. However, it seems to me that their practice separates the secular and the sacred. Instead, I would suggest that they both pray as he plays. That article led to the order of my book title, *Pray and Play*, since I believe that God wants us to bathe all of our actions, including our fun, in prayer to him, the 3-in-1 God of the Bible.

For example, Matt Jones won the 2014 Houston Open by chipping his golf ball into the hole from forty-two yards off the green, an amazing feat for which we can praise the Lord. The interesting report in the *Grand Rapids Press* by the Associated Press said that Matt told his caddy that he was going to do it. After remarking that Matt missed a disastrous putt last September, preventing him at that time from playing in the 2014 Masters Tournament, the reporter writes that "Destiny, however, had other plans for Jones...." My correction would be to replace the word "destiny" with "God," a substitution that would be much more accurate, biblically.

Watching other sports events

Now, you don't have to watch any of the games that I watch in order to benefit from the Bible passages and insights. For example, perhaps you enjoy watching sports in which your children or grandchildren participate. Always remember that God created the human bodies on both sides of those games, and that you can praise him for his display of his human handiwork and support your offspring at the same time. Remembering God's creation of those sports players' bodies can keep us from getting all worked up about who wins. Instead, praising God for the opposing players' abilities can help you keep a biblical perspective, even when you root for your teams. That insight has helped me root for the Chicago Cubs—even though they have not been baseball's champs since 1908. Next year!

The world's football

In the rest of the world outside of the U.S.A. and Canada, soccer, the world's "football," dominates sports fans' interests. My son-in-law, a medical doctor, is a fan of that kind of football, since he grew up in Kenya. However, I enjoy scoring in sports, and I find a 1-nil or nil-nil soccer game uninteresting.

Therefore, I came up with a solution to defensive, keep-away soccer games. I suggested to my son-in-law that they could have a four-minute shot clock that would require a team to make a shot on the other team's goal within four minutes of the time they get the ball, and that they should do away with the off-side rule, thus, producing more scoring in the games. However, he replied that he enjoys defensive soccer. It is true that God-given gifts of great skill are on display in that kind of football, especially since the players can't use their hands. Soccer and all fans can benefit from praising God for his gifts of both teams' talents in a match.

God's warning about dependence on humanity for our joy

In Jeremiah 17, God condemns his people's dependence on human strength and resources as follows: "This is what the LORD says, 'Cursed is the one who trusts in man, who depends on flesh for his strength and whose heart turns away from the LORD.... But blessed is the man who trusts in the LORD, whose confidence is in him....' The heart is deceitful above all things and beyond cure. Who can understand it? 'I the LORD search the heart and examine the mind, to reward a man according to his conduct.'" (verses 5, 7, 9–10). God also contrasts the permanent existence of the human who focuses on the LORD with the temporary life of the person who trusts only in human strength and abilities by comparing them to desert plants.

As I write these words, I'm watching an American Big Ten tournament basketball game, which shows both God's creative power in the teams' coaching and athletic abilities and human weaknesses in athletes' inability to score on more than 50 percent of their shots. Even the greatest American basketball player of all time, Michael Jordan, made slightly less than half of his career shots. However, he was at his best when the game was on the line late in the fourth quarter. With God's blessings of skillful bodies, pro sports stars make incredibly hard athletic actions look easy. The best players perform amazingly with relaxed muscles while experiencing the stress of a close game. We need to give God all the honor, since he made our bodies.

Many Christian believers fail to reflect on the sports events that they watch, as I used to do, and God's words in Jeremiah 17 are for them. Instead of accepting our culture's secular approach to sports, we need either to stop watching them or start praising the divine Creator for his might that is shown in them.

A New Testament passage about pleasure

Another Bible passage about the foolishness of focusing on human pleasure is Luke 12:16–21. Someone asks Jesus to arbitrate an inheritance between the speaker and his brother. Instead, Jesus warns his listeners about human greed by telling a parable about a rich man's greed after God blesses him with a huge crop. His responses are to build larger barns to store his wealth and to say to himself, "You have plenty of good things laid up for many years. Take life easy; eat, drink, and be merry." That same night, God takes his life from him. Thus, the purpose of our toil and fun as believers is to honor God, not to live selfishly.

Therefore, let's give our pleasurable sports events to God, who reveals his great power in such ways.

God's words to everyone about his creative power

The writer of the book of Ecclesiastes, Solomon, reflects on our relationship with our Creator, especially when we are young. He recommends the following to the younger generation: "Be happy, young man, while you are young, and let your heart give you joy in the days of your youth. Follow the ways of your heart and whatever your eyes see, but know that for all these things God will bring you to judgment. So, then, banish anxiety from your heart and cast off the troubles of your body, for youth and vigor are meaningless. Remember your Creator in the days of your youth, before the days of trouble come and the years approach when you will say, 'I find no pleasure in them.'... Fear God and keep his commandments, for this is the whole duty of man. For God will bring every deed into judgment, including every hidden thing, whether it is good or evil" (Ecclesiastes 11:9–10; 12:1, 13b–14).

Several comments about this passage apply to sports events, both for participants and spectators:

(1) Notice that wise Solomon calls on the younger generation to have fun but to consider that God will judge our motives and actions.

(2) Youthful activities are empty ("meaningless") and short-lived without God.

(3) The inspired writer commands everyone to "remember" our "Creator" when we are young, or our older years will tend to be meaningless, too.

(4) Remembering God as the one who made and enables our bodies to do fun activities means to obey and give him our honor and praise.

(5) Remembering in the Bible almost never means merely recalling God, but it has the meaning of obeying God's guidelines.

(6) The writer goes on to sum up his book in a command to fear God, a call to respect our Creator in all of our actions, including our fun.

(7) Inspired Solomon calls us to keep (obey) God's commandments. One of those is Paul's call to "rejoice in the Lord always," including during our pleasurable actions.

(8) Our life application must be to remember God, our Judge, since we will answer to him for every pleasurable thought and fun action at the Final Judgment after Jesus returns.

I just tuned in to the 2014 American NCAA men's basketball tournament, otherwise called "March Madness," to witness the end of fourteenth-seeded Mercer University's improbable, huge upset of second-seeded Duke University. In the post-game interview, the Mercer coach was understandably excited, to say the least. He then showed that he was not a victim of March Madness, but rather influenced by divine sanity, when he shouted into the microphone with a big smile, "Praise the Lord!" Those sentiments are mine exactly about "March Madness." Later, Tournament Central replayed that interview but edited out Bob Hoffman's "Praise the Lord!" Thus, you see the clash between human praise of the Creator and human secularism that ignores him.

If only we Christians were as bold as the Mercer coach to give credit to God for sports!

Personal experiences in basketball

I was tall when I was in high school and wanted to play basketball. However, when I was in grades eight and ten, I had foot trouble that kept me off the basketball team. As a result, my lack of experience held my career back. During grade eleven, I practiced on the opposite end of the court from the varsity team's play. In my senior year, the coach put me on the team for two-thirds of the home games, but I "collected splinters" on the bench.

However, toward the end of one game, when our team was far ahead, the crowd yelled, "Put Bruce in! Put Bruce in!" until my coach, to my surprise, obeyed their command during the other team's free throws with about thirty seconds left. When our team arrived at our end of the floor, I hustled to get free. With only five seconds left, one of our guards passed the ball to me near the fifteen-foot free-throw line. As I shot the ball, the game-ending buzzer went off. I missed the basket by about a foot—air ball! The team carried me off the floor on their shoulders anyway. Even though I missed the game-ending shot, the experience was still fun.

Many years later, when I coached seventh grade basketball during my last year of teaching, I decided to play all of my twenty-five players during nonconference games, even though our games were only twenty minutes long. We lost all of those contests, but my reasoning was that everyone should have the experience of competitive sports at least once.

In conference games, I played the top fourteen players who won five games and lost only three, tying another team for second place for which we received a trophy. We had two thrilling two-point victories in other schools' gymnasiums.

However, I was more thankful to God for the sportsmanship trophy that we won in an end-of-year tournament with seven teams from much larger schools.

It wasn't until after I became a pastor that God taught me through his Word, the Bible, to praise him for his creative power in sports instead of seeking selfish pleasure.

Bible Discussion Questions:

1. What do Genesis 2:7 and Psalm 139: 13–14 have to say to sports fans? Explain with specific examples from sports that you have witnessed.
2. What do you think about the pro baseball player's playing while his wife prays? What do you think about the author's reaction and his reversing the title of this book to *Pray and Play*? Why?
3. Read Jeremiah 17:5–10. How does the author apply this text to watching professional sports? How much do you agree with him? How will this passage affect your sports watching? Why?
4. Read Luke 12:16–21. What is the rich man's goal for his retirement? Why does God take his life away that same night? How can we avoid his punishment? Explain.
5. Read Ecclesiastes 11:9–12:14. How is the inspired writer's advice related to the topic of this book? Summarize his teachings and their application to sports.
6. How do you feel about the Mercer coach's outburst in that TV interview? What is your reaction to the author's playing and coaching experiences? Explain.

* * *

One Step on Our Journey with Jesus: Commit yourself to view sports with thoughts about God as the Creator of the human body. If you don't watch sports, commit every action to praise and pray to God.

* * *

With our eyes on our future prize, let's run Jesus' race while enjoying him during...

Chapter Nine

FAMILY EVENTS

God's pleasure in his family

The psalmist David, in Psalm 35:27–28, makes the following fascinating statement and call after wishing that God's justice be done to his enemies: "May those who delight in my vindication shout for joy and gladness; may they always say, 'The LORD be exalted, who delights in the well-being of his servant.' My tongue will speak of your righteousness and of your praises all day long." Notice that God's servant David and other believers are part of God's mutual-admiration society.

First of all, the LORD, Yahweh, experiences divine thrill in taking care of his willing servants. Second, his human family members delight in his many divine qualities in action. Third, those delivered believers call other followers to show their joy about God's loving activities. Fourth, God, through David, calls us to proclaim all of his delightful divine deeds in our lives as his adopted children by giving him all the credit.

Jeremiah 32:37b–41 also describes God's loving return of his human family to his Land of Promise, thus, replacing his justice in exiling them from his land with his mercy, "...I will bring them back to this place and let them live in safety. They will be my people, and I will be their God. I will give them singleness of heart so that they will always fear me for their own good and the good of their children after them. I will make an everlasting covenant with them: I will never stop doing good to them, and I will inspire them to fear me, so that they will never turn away from me. I will rejoice in doing them good and will assuredly plant them in this land with all my heart and soul."

Several comments about these verses come to mind:

(1) Notice that God's rescue is his doing, not ours. We only respond with faith, because he enables us to have "singleness of heart."

(2) His family relationship with us is repeated many times in the Bible. He is our God, and we are his people. This statement shows his covenant love for his human family members.

(3) Thus, people who use the phrase "my God" and other words like " hell" and "damn" meaninglessly as expressions of emotion are taking God's name in vain as they violate God's first commandment of ten: "You shall not misuse the name of the LORD your God, for the LORD will not hold anyone guiltless who misuses his name."

(4) In this way, all of the words we speak will be part of God's justice at the last day when Jesus issues his verdicts for all humans. The amazing fact is that we who trust in his life and death to get us

to heaven will hear God's final verdict of "not guilty" because of Jesus' death, not due to any actions or words of ours. However, if we merely stop using words that dishonor him without his change of our life to follow him and to want to be more like Jesus each day, we have not received his gift of new life.

(5) Notice also that his gift of eternity-enduring security in our lives has the result that we and our children will respect him. His covenant love in taking care of us extends to our whole family, not just us alone. If our descendants wander from God's path, we need to pray persistently that he will fulfill his promise. However, such unbelief in our children is part of the mystery of sin.

(6) When does God fulfill this wonderful picture of future bliss? It certainly doesn't come true after Israel returns from Babylon under King Cyrus, because even though they no longer worship idols of wood and stone, they increasingly rely on the law and their human-made rules to please God. During Jesus' time, the leaders put him to death because he threatens their legalistic control of the people, but they pay God's price for their rebellion with the Romans' destruction of Jerusalem in A.D. 70.

(7) Moreover, as we examine today's Israel, a vast majority of the Jews fail to trust in the God-man Jesus as God's only way to receive his love. Therefore, this passage will finally come true at a future date when Jesus comes back to give all true believers, not only Jews, perfect "singleness of heart" focusing on the

3-in-1 God. However, God's new birth has to happen in this life for his final perfection to come in the next.

When we examine the New Testament, we discover that God is only one God but also a Family of three Persons: the Father, Jesus, and the Holy Spirit. God's Word clearly reveals this truth at the prophet John's baptism of Jesus in Matthew 3:16–17: "As soon as Jesus was baptized, he went up out of the water. At that moment heaven was opened, and he saw the Spirit of God descending like a dove and lighting on him. And a voice from heaven said, 'This is my Son, whom I love; with him I am well pleased.'"

Similarly, the Father speaks about his heavenly pleasure in Jesus when he reveals his divine brightness in Jesus' body and in God's glowing glory cloud on the mountain to his followers Peter, James, and John, "This is my Son, whom I love; with him I am well-pleased. Listen to him" (Matthew 17:5b).

The astounding, mysterious truth of the Scriptures is that the one God in three Persons gladly welcomes me into his family as his adopted son. However, I will never become a god or a deity, since the Bible makes it clear that I'm a creature, not God, as some people believe. For example, inspired Paul writes, "Therefore, if anyone is in Christ, he is a new creation; the old has gone, the new has come." We believers become new creations, not gods, even though God fills us with his divine power through Jesus' mighty victory. The Bible always maintains the difference between the 3-in-1 God and us, his human creatures.

For example, our awesome God is everywhere-present, all-knowing, all-powerful, and eternal from the past to the future. We humans can never have those qualities of God.

I praise you, Father, Jesus, and Holy Spirit—one amazing God—for your willingness to adopt me even though I am totally unworthy!

Some family humor

All of the following family jokes came from the wealth of clean jokes at kcbx.net:

Unexpected guests were on the way; and my mother, an impeccable housekeeper, rushed around straightening up. She put my father and brother to work cleaning the guest bathroom.

Later, when she went to inspect it, she was surprised that the once-cluttered room had been tidied up so quickly. Then she saw the note on the closed shower curtains. It read, "Thank you for not looking in the bathtub."

Mary was having a tough day and had stretched herself out on the couch to do a bit of what she thought to be well-deserved complaining and self-pitying. She moaned to her mom and brother, "Nobody loves me, the whole world hates me!"

Her brother, busily occupied playing a game, hardly looked up at her and passed on this encouraging word: "That's not true, Mary. Some people don't even know you."

A young couple drove several miles down a country road, not saying a word. An earlier discussion had led to an argument, and neither wanted to concede their position. As they passed a barnyard of mules and pigs, the husband sarcastically asked, "Are they relatives of yours?"

"Yes," his wife replied. "I married into the family."

I ran short of money while visiting my brother and borrowed $50 from him. After my return home, I wrote him a short letter every few weeks, enclosing a $5 check in each one. He called me up and told me how much he enjoyed the letters, regardless of the money; I had never written regularly before. Eventually I sent off a letter and the last five-dollar check.

In my mail box the next week I found an envelope from my brother. Inside was another $50.

A large amount of humor points at human weaknesses, as these family jokes do. We laugh because we are weak, too, and recognize ourselves in those jokes. The last one pokes fun at our failure to communicate with our immediate family. How much more do we need to communicate with our heavenly Family, God, since Jesus has opened the path for us to enter the heavenly throne room through prayer twenty-four hours a day, seven days a week?

These jokes also gently make the point that all of our families were far from perfect. On the other hand, God's immediate divine "Family" is fully perfect. His 3-in-1 Family is worthy of our full devotion, prayers, and service as we joyfully serve our earthly related and nonrelated family. He deserves our most important loyalty.

Bible Discussion Questions:

1. Read Psalm 35:27–28 in the context of the whole psalm. Describe in your own words the "mutual admiration society" in those verses. How do you feel about that truth? Why?

2. Read Jeremiah 32:37–41. Which ones of the author's seven comments cause a response in you? State your positive or negative responses and your reasons for your reactions.
3. Why do you suppose that the cults and other religions have denied the biblical truth that God is one God in three Persons? Why can't people accept such a mystery? How much does God have to conform to our logic? Explain.
4. With which family joke do you identify the most? Why? What do you think about the author's comments about those jokes? Explain.

* * *

One Step on Our Journey with Jesus: Make an effort with prayer to mend any family rifts and lack of communication that have developed. Also, resolve to communicate more often with your heavenly Father through Jesus with the goal of fulfilling 1 Thessalonians 5:17, "Pray continually," in Jesus' great strength.

* * *

The Bible's divine priorities for our loyalties

According to Paul, our earthly loyalties to family and friends must take a backseat to our devotion to God. In 1 Corinthians 6:14, 16b, 18, God commands us through Paul, "Do not be yoked together with unbelievers. For what do righteousness and wickedness have in common?... For we are the temple of the living God. As God has said: 'I will live with them and walk among them, and I will be their God, and they will be my people....I will be a Father to you, and you will be my sons and daughters, says the Lord Almighty.'" Of course, this passage is about our relationships with unbelievers, but its truth can apply to all human relationships, which must never be as important as our covenant with God.

The reason I use the word "covenant" for our personal relationship with our divine Father, Jesus, and Holy Spirit is that Paul here quotes covenant language that God uses throughout the Old Testament for his ties with Israel. God says that he will be Israel's God and that they will be his people. Similarly, Paul, Peter, and John use those same words for New Testament believers from many nations and cultures—in other words, the church. It's the same covenant made with Abraham that is made into a new covenant in Jesus' life, death, and resurrection.

If you grew up in a committed Christian family, God made his covenant with that group. The children in your family were *under* all of God's covenant blessings of a Christian home and church. However, all family members who accept Jesus as the only Path to the Father's love and forgiveness are *in* the covenant by experiencing him personally.

Another Bible passage that's shocking to some people is Mark 3:20–21, 31–35, "Then Jesus entered a house, and again a crowd gathered, so that he and his disciples were not even able to eat. When his family heard about this, they went to take charge of him, for they said, 'He is out of his mind'…. Then Jesus' mother and brothers arrived. Standing outside, they sent someone in to call him. A crowd was sitting around him, and they told him, 'Your mother and brothers are outside looking for you.' 'Who are my mother and brothers,' he asked. Then he looked at those seated in a circle around him and said, 'Here are my mother and my brothers. Whoever does God's will is my brother and sister and mother.'"

(1) Family can be our idol by depending on our relatives more than we do God. Perhaps one way to measure our competing loyalties is to ask ourselves, "Who would I rather talk to when life gets stressful—God, a family member, or a friend?" Of course, God can use such people to support and comfort us, but he's the one doing it through them. Prayer must be our first avenue to stress relief.

(2) Jesus' family hear that he is so busy teaching and healing people that he skips meals.

(3) As a result, they determine to "take charge of him." That action in the original Greek means to "arrest" him. Family members sometimes want to control our actions and decisions.

(4) When his mother and brothers arrive, expecting Jesus to drop everything and come to them, they get a shock when he fails to obey them.

(5) His response may seem harsh, but Jesus has a choice to knuckle under to his family's control or to obey his heavenly Father by continuing his ministry.

(6) Jesus' statement that the people sitting in a circle around him, who are listening eagerly to his teaching, are his mother and brothers reveals his perfect decision to be faithful to his heavenly Father's ministry more than his relatives' desires.

(7) Thus, our pleasure must the by-product of our surrender to God rather than to humans. In this way, our obedience to humans must happen, because God wants us to submit to human authority. Again, like Jesus' submission to the authorities' capital punishment, our desires must focus on God and God alone. Then he will lift up our emotions with his gift of joy in Jesus.

In addition, a Bible passage referring to Jesus' joy and his enduring the cruel, criminal cross is Hebrews 12:2. After calling us to persevere in running our race toward God, the writer to the Hebrews encourages us, "Let us fix our eyes on Jesus, the author and perfecter of our faith, who for the joy set before him endured the cross, scorning its shame, and sat down at the right hand of the throne of God." For our purposes, the source of Jesus' joy about and motive for enduring the extreme pain and suffering of the Roman torture instrument are to look beyond his death when he will reenter heaven to rule the universe with the Father. His joy even in the middle of his suffering can be the source of our God-centered pleasure even during life's reverses.

Therefore, our pleasure through Jesus' victorious power must also motivate our obedience to our Father's will with genuine thanks.

Notice also that Jesus begins and completes our faith. As a result, we can claim no credit for our increasing pleasure in God, who receives 100 percent of the honor.

God's will for our family time

So far, we have seen that God wants us to avoid idolizing our family. However, this question arises: what is our responsibility toward our immediate relatives? Jesus' Sermon on the Mount gives us guidance for our relationships with them. In Matthew 5:14, 16, he teaches us, "You are the light of the world.... Let your light shine before men, that they may see your good deeds and praise your Father in heaven." Thus, Jesus' challenge is that we become his agents of light to our family by listening to and lovingly serving them, rather than gaining selfish pleasure from family events.

You see, our focus has to shift from our selfish family fun to the pleasure of unselfish service for the good of our loved ones.

I didn't experience an emotionally close family in my childhood. Our emotional distance created a lot of loneliness in my life, which Jesus filled up when he began my faith at the age of sixteen. When we have a close, loving family during our youth, the advantage is that we may experience God's unconditional love through our parents and siblings. However, often, when emotional, physical, or sexual abuse happen, we harbor inner wounds that only God can heal through professional people who enable us to express our real emotions about our broken family.

Sometimes, such childhood abuse can rob us of gladly responding to God's joy that he feels toward us.

Bible Discussion Questions:
1. Read 1 Corinthians 6:14–18. How can we be separate from unbelievers while still witnessing to them, as God's Word calls us to do? What does Paul mean by saying that we must avoid being unequally yoked with unbelievers? How can we build bridges to other people without being influenced by their sinful values and lifestyles? Explain.
2. Read Mark 3:20–21, 31–35. What does this passage say about our relationships with our families? Which of the author's comments help your Christian life the most? Explain.
3. Read Hebrews 12:2 in its context. How can Jesus experience joy as he faces the excruciating pain and suffering of the cross? How can we also find pleasure in God as we suffer? What experiences has God given you of his love and grace while you suffered? Explain.
4. How can we be God's light to our families, as Jesus describes in Matthew 5:14–16? To other nearby people? Give specific examples of actions that you can do to have Jesus' light shining through you to others.

* * *

One Step on Our Journey with Jesus: Meditate on this section's Bible passages for several days. Ask God for Jesus' victory to put them into practice for his praise and pleasure. When he gives you spiritual progress, share his work in your life with people

near you, remembering to give him your honor for changing you through Jesus' victory.

* * *

As we seek Jesus' joy on our joyful journey toward our final reward, let's consider...

Chapter Ten

Participation Sports

God's pleasure in human humility, not abilities

To determine God's opinion about hobbies and organized sports in which we participate, we need to go to Psalm 147, a praise poem in the original Hebrew language. The unnamed psalmist starts with "Praise the LORD" or "Hallelujah!" Recently, two different times, I sat in church behind two boys when we sang songs using that latter call to praise God.

After the services, I asked those young men if they knew what "hallelujah" meant. Neither one did. Then I told them that it meant "Praise the LORD." I think that sometimes we assume that younger people always understand the need to lift God up in worship. Even more, we assume that we are honoring God in our good, clean fun, because it isn't forbidden in the Scriptures.

However, how often do we think about God during our hunting, fishing, snow and water sports, golf, tennis, sewing, quilting, board and card games, dominoes, collecting of objects, and other hobbies and participation games?

The psalmist continues in 147:1, "How good it is to sing praises to our God; how pleasant and fitting to praise him." As we lift God's great name with honor to him all the time, he lifts up our spirits to feel his constant joy. In fact, such a lifting up of our human spirits with our focus on God is the meaning of joy in the Bible.

The psalmist goes on to give our amazing Creator praise for maintaining his creation. Then in verses 10 and 11, he writes, "His pleasure is not in the strength of the horse, nor his delight in the legs of a man; the LORD delights in those who fear him, who put their hope in his unfailing love."

Notice that God doesn't feel joy about his creatures' abilities, but takes pleasure in our focus on him in all of our activities, including our participation in hobbies and sports.

However, someone might think that God's joy in our praising him is self-centered. On the contrary, he is the only one worthy of anyone's honor. All humans are imperfect, but he is perfect in every way. When we remember him with joyful praise in church, and all the time, we are merely doing what we were created to do—acknowledge his creative power as our Maker.

For example, we play dominoes with a church group. God has taught me to praise him for his guidance of the dominoes that I draw even though they might be high numbers leading to a high score that loses the game.

How can I praise God even when I lose a game? I joyfully observe how he guides some other players' success. Also, God teaches me patience and submission to his will when I lose and humility when I win, because he guides his creation, even in domino games, as the psalmist declares.

God's point through the psalmist is that he is thrilled with our respect (fear) and hopeful focus on his awesome love as we pray and play our hobbies and sports.

For example, Jeremiah, in chapter 9, calls the Israelites to lament God's coming punishment for their rebellion against him, which is also shown by today's secular cultures' love of pleasure. Secularism can also influence Christians' thinking about their fun. I'm fearful that the secularism of our culture's schools and media has influenced our youth and adults to separate God from fun.

Then God inspires Jeremiah to write, "This is what the LORD says, 'Let not the wise man boast of his wisdom or the strong man boast of his strength or the rich man boast of his riches…'" (verse 22). God's Word makes it clear that our culture's secular focus on our hobbies and sports and on "worshiping" celebrated humans' abilities not only disregards him as our Creator and Maintainer, but also spawns real rebellion against him.

God's pleasure in his faithful people

Then Jeremiah quotes God in chapter 9, verse 23, "'...But let him who boasts boast about this, that he understands and knows me, that I am the LORD, who exercises kindness, justice, and righteousness on earth, for in these I delight,' declares the LORD." Notice that God's focus is not the typical human emphasis on admiring human abilities, but instead on enabling us to "understand and know" him. Furthermore, we need to focus our thoughts and joyful feelings on his many divine qualities like "kindness, justice, and righteousness."

In other words, God is favorably disposed toward us but justly and rightly has to punish human sinful rebellion like secularism. How can we who are guilty escape his discipline? All Christians should know that we can't deny or avoid God's justice against our natural rebellion. Instead, Jesus satisfies God's justice by living a perfect life and dying in our place on the cross. It's only through Jesus' divine human actions that God forgives us. He not only enables us to trust in Jesus as our Substitute, but also empowers us to follow Jesus with our increasing focus on him and his will. As a result, he gives us the new birth to "understand and know" him.

Thus, we have nothing about which to brag, but God creates and rescues us with his unlimited power. All the credit goes to our 3-in-1 God.

For example, I enjoy a half-hour of swimming laps at a local indoor pool every weekday it's open. A doctor told me that swimming exercises every muscle in our bodies, except one—the coccyx muscle at the bottom of the spine. Since I swim on my back with my ears just below the water's surface, I can't communicate with anyone as I swim. Therefore, my swimming time has become my prayer time alone with God, enjoying him.

Humorous human weakness

The following human gaffes are from kcbx.net, a great collection of clean jokes:

"We now have exactly the same situation as we had at the start of the race, only exactly the opposite." (Murray Walker)

After playing Cameroon in the 1990 World Cup finals, Bobby Robson said, "We didn't underestimate them. They were just a lot better than we thought."

On the difficulties of adjusting to playing football or soccer and living in Italy: "It was like being in a foreign country." (Ian Rush)

Jimmy Hill: "Don't sit on the fence, Terry. What chance do you think Germany has of getting through?"

Terry Venables: "I think it's 50-50."

"I was in a no-win situation, so I'm glad that I won rather than lost." (Frank Bruno)

"There's going to be a real ding-dong when the bell goes." (David Coleman)

"There is Brendan Foster by himself with 20,000 people." (David Coleman)

"The lead car is absolutely unique, except for the one behind it which is identical." (Murray Walker)

"I owe a lot to my parents, especially my mother and father." (Golfer Greg Norman)

"There have been injuries and deaths in boxing, but none of them serious." (Alan Minter)

Bible Discussion Questions:
1. Read Psalm 147. What verses in this psalm can we apply to our hobbies and participation sports and activities? How can they be applied to our lives?
2. What do you think about the author's explanation of the fact that God's pleasure in our praise of him is not self-centered? Why?
3. How did this chapter change your view about participation in hobbies and sports? Explain.
4. Read Jeremiah 9:22–23 in the context of the whole chapter. How do these verses contradict the usual human way of looking at participation hobbies and sports? Why?
5. How do the sports jokes point up human weakness in the sports world? Why do we laugh? Explain.

* * *

One Step on Our Journey with Jesus: Take one pleasurable activity and surrender it to praising God for his creative power and mighty guidance. Then give another one to your great Creator in prayer and praise. Finally, give all of your tasks to God and praise him for his divine power as you do them. Then share his work in your life with others.

* * *

As we take our terrific trip toward God's gift of our final inheritance, we examine our...

Chapter Eleven

USE OF ELECTRONIC DEVICES AND THE INTERNET

Several people have told me that their electronic devices and the Internet are addictive. What is God's will for our use of them?

God's pleasure about his universe described in Psalm 24 and Genesis 1

In Psalm 24, when David expresses his utter joy at the transportation of the Ark of the Covenant, the symbol of God's powerful presence among his people, to God's earthly capital city, he couples God's ownership of everyone with the true reason we honor him—his creation of humanity. He begins the psalm with a reference to the only true God: "The earth is the LORD's and everything in it, the world and all who live in it; for he founded it upon the seas and established it upon the waters" (verses 1–2).

Similarly, in Genesis chapter 1, God pronounces all that he has made "very good" (Genesis 1:31). I believe that these descriptions depict God's joy in his creation.

Thus, he owns our electronic devices and has provided them for our enjoyment of him and as tools to make our lives more meaningful and productive for his praise. As with any other part of his creation, humans tend to divorce the true God of the Bible from their electronic devices and let them become addictive idols to which they become attached. Instead of controlling electronic devices, humans tend to let their electronic environment control them.

Then David, in Psalm 24:3–6, describes the right-living person who will enter the holy place to be with God: "Who may ascend the hill of the LORD? Who may stand in his holy place? He who has clean hands and a pure heart, who does not lift up his soul to an idol or swear by what is false. He will receive blessing from the LORD and vindication from God his Savior. Such is the generation of those who seek him, who seek your face, O God of Jacob." I feel that God wants me to make several observations about this passage:

(1) Who of us can claim that we have completely clean hearts before God? Only Jesus throughout his life led such a life.
(2) Thus, the only way we can enter God's holy place in heaven is through Jesus' perfectly obedient life, death as our Substitute, and re-entry into heaven. We can only go there in prayer through Jesus' victory for us.
(3) Therefore, God the Father accepts us only by looking at Jesus' perfect actions in our place.

(4) As a result, in the light of the New Testament, the committed believer that David describes is not perfect but receives Jesus' perfection to pray to and live in the presence of the holy God.

(5) David also describes true believers as those who seek God. We must examine our use of electronic devices to see if we seek Internet information and connections with other people more than we seek God in prayer. If seeking God is second or third place behind electronic devices or the Internet, we need to seek God's fruit of the Spirit of self-control to replace our self-centered impulsiveness (Galatians 5:22–23).

(6) God, through Jesus, can give us his powerful rescue as our Savior or Deliverer from electronic-device addiction, through which the devil tries to distract us from praying to the true God.

(7) On a personal note, in my high school speech class, I read Psalm 24 when I had to do a dramatic reading before the court decisions that banished God and the Christian faith from public school classrooms. Instead, the religion of secular humanism has dominated public education and has influenced many Christians.

In fine, inspired, poetic form, David writes, "Lift up your heads, O you gates; be lifted up, you ancient doors, that the King of glory may come in. Who is this King of glory? The LORD strong and mighty, the LORD mighty in battle. Lift up your heads, O you gates; lift them up, you ancient doors, that the King of glory may come in.

Who is he, this King of glory? The LORD Almighty—he is the King of glory" (Psalm 24:7–10).

(1) As with any addiction, electronic devices can control us, but who's strong enough to defeat the devil's desire to control us through them and other idols? We can't in our own strength, but God can through Jesus' victory.

(2) David says that God is mighty in battle. In his day, God commissions him to conquer the rest of the Promised Land that the people of Israel, under the Judges, have failed to control.

(3) However, as Paul states clearly in Ephesians 6:10–12, our fight is not against humans, but against the spiritual evil forces that tempt us to make electronic devices and the Internet our idols that, in turn, control us.

(4) God is "the King of glory" who dwells in bright divine light that the Israelites experience with God's presence in a fiery pillar that leads them for forty years in the Sinai desert and which Peter, James, and John see displayed in Jesus on the mountain when God shows them Jesus' divine brightness or glory.

(5) Furthermore, the Gospel of John says that Jesus' death on the cruel, criminal cross is his gory glory.

(6) When we "lift up our heads" to let him control our electronics, he then can guide us to his victory to use our devices as tools for his praise.

(7) He will then "enter" our lives, so that we can seek God in their use. Such electronic use pleases him.

Human pleasure in using electronic devices

Pleasure in anything can lead to an addiction or idolatry. A quick Internet search on my favorite engine, dogpile.com, yields a number of articles and blogs about electronic-device addiction.

I saw an example of electronic-device addiction at the indoor swimming pool. A young father who brought his two children to the pool spent about fifteen minutes of my swim immersed constantly in his handheld device. His daughter and son came over to him, and they all decided to leave. Before they got to the other side of the pool near the locker-room doors, he again stood still with his head down, looking at his phone. A few minutes later, he and his children were standing near the front desk, with his wrapt attention again glued to his cell phone. He again stopped before he exited the front door, while his kids fooled around waiting for him. I just hoped that he didn't get his children in an accident driving home while using his device.

To illustrate the young father's experience, at prioritylearningresearch.com, in an article entitled, "Are You Addicted To Your Electronic Devices?" the writer says, "These devices are considered 'psychoactive,' meaning that using them can alter our mood and create pleasurable feelings. We enjoy getting emails, text messages, and social networking site updates, but we never know when they are coming. This often causes us to check our phones constantly."

The writer lists three indications that we are addicted:

(1) You are staying up too late using devices.
(2) Your device use has unintended consequences in your family life. (In other words, your children and spouse show signs that you are not focusing on them but on your device.)
(3) Your electronic device use is creating a potentially dangerous situation (for example, if you are texting or talking on the cell phone while driving).

The two bits of advice that the writer suggests to remedy the addiction follow:

(1) Realize that the world won't end if you don't pick up your phone.
(2) Set aside some time to get unplugged.

Stay tuned for my spiritual, not humanistic, suggestions.

Another clever article, "The 12 Step E-Tox: How To Curb Your Electronic Device," at huffingtonpost.com, recommends "e-tox" rather than detox for electronic-device addiction. The writer, who was deeply addicted to her cell phone, describes the turning point. "This past January, I hit bottom. On a short vacation to the beach with my kids, I found myself running back to the hotel room for 'sunscreen' when a full bottle was right there next to me and dashing out of the pool anytime I heard a blip (even if it wasn't mine). It was pathetic, but I couldn't stop myself. That is, until my 7-year-old daughter asked if I'd pleeease turn off my phone for the rest of the weekend and started to cry. It was then I knew I needed an e-tox."

Then follows the writer's twelve-step e-tox program parallel to the Alcoholics Anonymous "detox" program:

(1) Admit you have a problem, not just to yourself, but also to your family who can help you stay on the right path.
(2) Decide when to start, perhaps on a vacation.
(3) Set reasonable parameters. Decide on giving up your device for a whole weekend, for example, instead of avoiding it "cold turkey."
(4) Accept withdrawal "pains."
(5) Do a reality check. For example, tell yourself that you're not really as important as you thought you were.
(6) Take personal inventory. Examine why you need to be glued to your device. Perhaps a mental health professional could help you sort out why you need to use your phone almost constantly.
(7) Reconnect with your body. Get regular exercise without e-interference.
(8) Make amends. Apologize to people affected by your addiction.
(9) Set car rules. The writer put her phone in her purse and locked it in her trunk.
(10) Reintroduce it gradually. After an e-less weekend, the writer found more control over her cell phone on Monday.
(11) Allow for regression. Let your conscience and family help you overcome temptation.
(12) Find a new normal.

However, this twelve-step program doesn't even mention our need for a "Higher Power" to help us, unlike Alcoholics Anonymous' plan.

Similarly, the trouble with most of these self-help approaches is that they depend on human effort in human strength like New Year's resolutions. Since Satan uses such devices to distract us from God, he is much stronger than we are in our own power. However, God's power, which is much stronger than he is, can enable us to control our electronics as tools, not as obsessive objects.

For example, I found that when my e-mails and the Internet took too much time away from my writing ministry, I resolved to God, through prayer, to look at them and to read the local newspaper online for forty-five minutes, with the deadline of our evening meal to end it.

God's estimation of a culture's love of pleasure

Paul writes to his fellow pastor Titus about the tempter's tempting tendency in Titus 3:3, "At one time we too were foolish, disobedient, deceived and enslaved by all kinds of passions and pleasures." He combines love of fun with hatred, malice, and envy in the next verse. God's Word makes fun-loving just as much a sin as other ones that we usually recognize as evil.

Certainly, if Paul were writing today under God's inspiration, he would include our culture's electronic-device idolatry in his list of evils.

Believers' fun focusing on God with their use of electronics

As with all of the other pleasures in my book, I don't recommend complete abstinence. Instead, I suggest dependence on God's strength through Jesus' awesome victory to control our use of fun activities. As a result, Paul, in Titus chapter 3, contrasts human selfishness with Christians' new life as follows: "But when the kindness and love of God our Savior appeared, he saved us, not because of righteous things we had done, but because of his mercy. He saved us through the washing of rebirth and renewal by the Holy Spirit, whom he poured out on us generously through Jesus Christ our Savior, so that, having been justified by his grace, we might become heirs having the hope of eternal life" (Titus 3:4–8).

This meaningful passage prompts several observations:

(1) God rescues us from our selfish, unbelieving lives with which we are born and empowers us, in Jesus Christ, to refocus our lives on him.

(2) We can do nothing to earn or merit God's deliverance, which only comes from his great love and kindness, for which we are completely undeserving.

(3) Notice that the Father, Jesus, and the Holy Spirit as our one God are all involved in our spiritual rescue.

(4) He also justifies us--that is, declares us "not guilty" as our Judge and right with him—not because of us, but because of Jesus' life, death, and resurrection.

(5) Furthermore, another amazing teaching is that God makes us heirs of the future new universe under Jesus.

(6) Finally, God's revealing of his unlimited, generous kindness, love, mercy, and Holy Spirit renewal provokes our thankfulness and praise in the use of God's pleasurable gifts.

Thus, as God's adopted inheritors of his future new creation, how can we let the creation—for example, electronic devices—control us? In his strength, we can break free of the creation's and Satan's control in this and other forms of pleasure. God's ways for guiding us are very different from the above humanistic ways to break free from the idolatry of fun—in this case, electronic-device addiction.

The Christian life often boils down to the need for balance among all of God's priorities and saying "no" to the comparatively unimportant activities. Thus, what does God want in our choices? Well, he makes dependent prayer a high priority, along with work and family. Electronic fun is down the list.

Having written that truth, I'm very thankful for God's gift of the Internet and my desktop computer as his tools for my writing ministry. However, we don't own smart phones, only dumb phones!

Bible Discussion Questions:

1. Read Psalm 24 and Genesis 1:31. List all of the ways you can think of that God's creation changed because of Adam and Eve's sinful rebellion against him. In what ways do we struggle with our fallen bodies and the world around us? How have you experienced God's ownership of his world? Explain.
2. Read Titus 3:1–8. How do you feel about Paul's teachings in these verses? Explain. What do you think about the author's applications of these passages to the uses of electronic devices? Why?

3. How are the Christians' ways of overcoming addiction to pleasure different from those of non-Christians (described in this chapter)? How is our motivation different from unbelievers? Explain.
4. How will you change the ways that you use electronic devices as a result of your Bible discussion? Why?

* * *

One Step on Our Journey with Jesus: Decide to pray persistently to the 3-in-1 God for Jesus' victory over your inappropriate use of electronic devices, if you have that problem at all. Listen for his guidance and follow it in curbing that addiction or idolatry. If you don't have such an addictive pleasure, praise him that he has spared you from it. If you use electronic devices, pray to God before and after you use them, as with any concentrated action.

* * *

As we limp along the rocky path toward final resurrection perfection, let's consider…

Chapter Twelve
HOBBIES, MUSIC, AND SPECIAL INTERESTS

God's pleasure in his creation

Throughout the last twenty-six chapters of the book of Isaiah, God often describes his creative power in making the earth and the rest of the universe. For example, Isaiah preaches, "For this is what the LORD [Yahweh] says—he who created the heavens, he is God; he who fashioned and made the earth, he founded it; he did not create it to be empty, but formed it to be inhabited—he says: 'I am the LORD, and there is no other'" (45:18), especially compared to all of the false gods concocted by the human mind, behind which are the evil beings tempting us to take our attention away from the true Creator God.

Humans' central, false god is self.

Such teachings in the Bible about our all-powerful Maker directly contradict human ideas saying that the universe all came by chance or that it just developed and grew by itself. Our divine Designer is all-knowing in his amazing manufacture of life in his creation. I am also in awe of his greatness that fills his universe and that is beyond it.

God is a constructing deity, and he has given us creativity, too. For example, we attended a Grand Rapids, Michigan, U.S.A., Symphony concert of Ludwig van Beethoven's amazing compositions, including his seventh symphony. In the conductor's educational, preconcert talk, he described the seventh symphony as Beethoven's most joyful composition, in fact, probably the most joyful one in all of music.

You must understand that Beethoven was deaf when he composed that symphony, which was probably written for his mysterious woman friend.

However, writing about Beethoven, the pantheism-index.com website claims, "This great musician abandoned the Catholicism of his upbringing and adopted Goethe's Pantheism." Several writers have asserted that he was a pantheist; that is, someone who equates the universe with God, like the six *Star Wars* movies (the "Force"). In other words, pantheism believes that God is the same as the universe, not that God made the universe.

Thus, we need to make a decision between God's statements and human ideas about the divine and choose God's teachings about his creation and ownership of our pleasure.

On the other hand, in spite of Beethoven's false ideas about God and his human weaknesses, God's greatness shines abundantly through his music with its great power and harmony. Praise the Creator!

Human pleasure in creativity

God, in his Word, the Bible, paints a dark picture of human pleasure that doesn't give credit to him as the Creator. For instance, in Isaiah 45:16, two verses before the one that asserts God's creation of all things, Isaiah says about idol-makers, "All the makers of idols will be put to shame and disgraced; they will go off into disgrace together." Similarly, all celebrity worship of movie and sports stars, as well as of royal personalities, is in the same category. Just because people are rich and famous doesn't mean that they are any happier with the permanent joy that only God can give us.

Someone might say that God is a little too hard on humans, but he is brutally honest about our lost birth status. However, we are the Evil One's slaves when we are born into this life, whether we are "good" people or not. In slavery to self and Satan, our focus is on ourselves and other people in our pleasurable activities rather than on God as our Creator.

Thus, as Christians, God calls us to divorce our pleasure from our selfish happiness and to flee to him as the Source of our deep-down joy in his creation.

Another Bible passage that can be applied to hobbies, music, and other interests is Ecclesiastes 2:8–11: "I amassed silver and gold for myself and the treasure of kings and provinces. I acquired men and women singers, and a harem as well—the delights of the heart of man. I became greater by far than anyone in Jerusalem before me. In all this, my wisdom stayed with me. I denied myself nothing my eyes desired. I refused my heart no pleasure. My heart took delight in all my work, and this was the reward for all my labor. Yet when I surveyed all that my hands had done and what I had toiled to achieve, everything was meaningless, a chasing after the wind; nothing was gained under the sun."

In thinking about Solomon's writing, a few observations come to mind:

(1) What are we working so hard for? I already cited a tavern or pub near us that brags about having the longest "happy hour" of four hours. I saw their electronic sign this week also boasting that they have thirty-two kinds of beer. I guess that if you drink eight kinds of beer an hour, you can taste all of them in that "happy hour." However, you wouldn't have such a "happy hour" the following morning.

My point is that some people work really hard for a "happy hour" or a "happy weekend" in order to escape their sad, meaningless reality. Such is sinful human escapism.

(2) People in developed countries have disposable income with which to experience either meaningful or meaningless pleasurable pursuits. Solomon calls all such activities that are divorced from God as "meaningless, a chasing after the wind."

(3) Working hard for God is meaningful to him and should also be for us as believers. Pleasure done for him is also meaningful,

as long as such pleasure doesn't interfere with our other responsibilities in relationship with God and people in our lives.

(4) Solomon also makes the point that human pleasure "under the sun"—in other words, done without any thought of God but only for selfish fun—is only temporary, like "chasing after the wind," a totally-futile attempt to have permanent meaning.

(5) The word "meaningless" in the original Hebrew language means an exhaled breath. We can't catch our breath or the wind, but the human race runs after selfish pleasures. However, they can't quite catch them as permanent fixtures of life. Instead, people keep trying but never succeed.

(6) Focusing on God, our Creator, in our fun and all of life brings deep, satisfying meaning to our lives.

(7) God has blessed some people with more money than we need so that we can use it to benefit others, and such thankful unselfishness for God's honor brings deep, long-lasting pleasure.

When the American singing-contest TV show *American Idol* began, I felt that God wanted me to preach a message series entitled "American Idols." I based the series on Bible texts that point out that human-centered pleasure of adoring people's talents without giving credit to their Source is idolatry. That series also pointed out the many other American idols that distract us from the only living God of the Bible.

Bible Discussion Questions:
1. Read Isaiah 45:16–19. What are the differences between idols and the true God? What evidence of his creative power do you see around you in his world? What is the deception of pleasure-seekers' worship of fun? Explain.
2. You don't have to like classical music to appreciate the author's point about Beethoven's reason and genius for composing his music. What is the author's emphasis? Do you agree that humans often honor celebrities without thinking about their Creator? Why?
3. Read Ecclesiastes 2:1–11. Which ones of the author's seven comments on these verses are especially meaningful to you? Why?
4. What kind of music do you enjoy? How can you listen to it meaningfully with God in mind? Explain.

* * *

One Step on Our Journey with Jesus: Examine the kind of music that you enjoy. Find some way to honor God, the Creator of music, as you listen to it. If you can't, find the kind with which you can praise him. Do the same thing with your honor of celebrities, if you do. Honor the God who gave them their talents or status with your thoughts, as you think about them.

* * *

When we return to Isaiah 45, we see that the prophet quotes our Creator God's plea to humanity in verses 22–25, "'Turn to me and be saved, all you ends of the earth; for I am God, and there is no other. By myself I have sworn; my mouth has uttered in all integrity a word that will not be revoked. Before me every knee will bow; by me every tongue will swear. They will say of me, 'In the LORD alone are righteousness and strength.' All who have raged against him will come to him and be put to shame. But in the LORD all the descendants of Israel will be found righteous and will exalt." Several comments about this passage follow:

(1) Notice that God pleads with us to lift him up as the Creator-Deliverer of his rescued people.

(2) Some people have imagined that all humans will go to heaven as it appears to happen with every knee bending to acknowledge that he is the only true God. However, the prophet's comment after God's call shows that many people who fail to lift God up as their Maker-Rescuer "will be put to shame."

(3) As a result, human repentance ("Turn to me") is necessary for our entrance to final life with God.

(4) However, we can't rescue ourselves. Only Jesus' death overcomes our shame.

(5) Thus, our need to present our experiences with the true God to people around us is great, since God himself calls all people to himself and because he wants us to point other people to him as our Deliverer.

(6) Both believers and unbelievers will bow before God when Jesus returns, but the former will do it genuinely from their hearts.

However, unbelievers will bend their knees reluctantly and then will experience, sadly, eternal separation from God in hell.

(7) God is the only Source of "righteousness and strength" through Jesus' life, death, and resurrection. Thus, we need to focus on him in our enjoyment of hobbies, music, and special interests, just as the passage describes believers' exalting him even as they lower themselves "bending their knees."

The death of secular thinking ignoring God

We now turn to another remarkable Old Testament passage, the last words of the prophet Zechariah in chapter 14: "On that day HOLY TO THE LORD will be inscribed on the bells of the horses, and the cooking pots in the LORD's house will be like the sacred bowls in front of the altar. Every pot in Jerusalem and Judah will be holy to the LORD Almighty, and all who come to sacrifice will take some of the pots and cook in them. And on that day there will no longer be a Canaanite in the house of the LORD Almighty" (verses 20–21). Notice the following comments about this passage:

(1) God commands that Moses write the words "HOLY TO THE LORD" on the high priest's turban to set him apart to lead the people's worship, whereas in this passage, the same words will be on the horses' bells.

(2) Thus, he emphasizes that all of life is holy (set apart as worship) to the true God, even the symbols of luxury, the horses' bells (and, for example, all of our pleasurable activities).

(3) The Old Testament law describes God's sacred objects in the place of worship, but all of his people's pots will be sacred.

In other words, every aspect of life is to be set apart for our worship of the 3-in-1 God, who now calls us to do away with our secular thinking.

(4) Our ridding of our secularism to make all of life sacred anticipates Jesus' Second Coming "on that day."

(5) The "sacrifices" that we offer today are not slaughtered animals, but our lives as "living sacrifices" (Romans 12:1–2).

(6) When Jesus returns, the Canaanites (all unbelievers) will be banished after his Final Judgment, when he will declare all of his true followers "not guilty" because of their faith in his sacrificial death to pave their way to the heavenly Father.

(7) My conclusion from these verses for our study is that all of our fun must be dedicated to the LORD of creation who gives us Jesus Christ's triumph.

The author's personal witness to God's work in his life

When I became a Christian (see *Doubtbusters! God Is My Shrink!*), I discovered the biblical words of Handel's oratorio, *Messiah*, which the composer wrote in three weeks for the secular reason of making money. I marveled at the soaring choruses lifting our Creator-Rescuer up in Jesus the Messiah's triumph.

God then used a music-appreciation class in college to help me appreciate classical music's harmony and power, especially with the musical genius of Beethoven, Mozart, Dvorak, Brahms, and Tchaikovsky, as played by symphony orchestras.

Today, as I listen to classical music in live performances and as a background for my writing, I rejoice in the God who enabled composers to write such amazing music and who enables people to make musical instruments "sing" harmoniously.

You have to understand that after six weeks of my fumbling, musical attempts, my piano teacher said bluntly, "You're a lost cause!" Musical talent does not run in our family. Therefore, I greatly admire God, who gave composers, conductors, and players their talents.

Thus, throughout that Grand Rapids (Michigan) Symphony Orchestra Beethoven performance, I praised the Creator for his creative power in Beethoven's creation of powerful, melodious, joyful music.

Of course, neither the composers Handel and Beethoven nor the players may have had God-honoring motives in mind for their composing and playing, but I'm thankful that God has taught me to praise him for the astounding results of their imperfect, fallen attempts at making music. In fact, all of our objects of pleasure are far from perfect, but God calls us to honor him as his creative power shines through them in spite of their weaknesses.

Another Bible passage instructing us about fun

That truth comes through in Psalm 19 about the two ways God shows us himself in his creation. The psalmist exclaims, "The heavens declare the glory of God; the skies proclaim the work of his hands.... The law of the LORD is perfect, reviving the soul.... Who can discern his errors? Forgive my hidden faults. Keep your servant also from willful sins; may they not rule over me. Then will I be blameless, innocent of great transgression. May the words of my mouth and the meditation of my heart be pleasing in your sight, O LORD, my Rock and my Redeemer" (verses 1, 7, 12–14).

We need to meditate on this passage for a while:

(1) Notice, first of all, that one way God reveals himself (his "glory" [his brightly-shining nature]) to all creatures is by the universe, earth, and people around us.

(2) The whole creation has become tarnished with the self-centered rebellion of humans, but God's greatness shines through it anyway.

(3) The second way God reveals his divine nature is through his Word, the Bible, which, according to the psalmist, is our contact lenses clarifying God's greatness in his world.

(4) The inspired psalmist, David, prays for God to cleanse his life from outer, obvious, inner, and invisible imperfections. Our prayers should be the same to prevent us from adopting the secular values of a fun-loving culture.

(5) Being "blameless" is to avoid major visible flaws of character that would bring dishonor to God. It does not mean being completely perfect. I believe that such perfection will only happen to us when we ditch these imperfect bodies at death or at the resurrection of our bodies.

(6) The purpose of this book is to help you meditate on your pleasurable times biblically (verse 14), so that God may rejoice in your words and thoughts.

Bible Discussion Questions:
1. Read Isaiah 45:22–25. Which ones of the author's comments about these verses stand out to you the most? Why?
2. How is true repentance different from feeling sorry for your sins? What must you do for your repentance to be pleasing to God? Explain.
3. Read Zechariah 14:20–21. Summarize the main point of those verses. How does God's point apply to your fun? Explain how these verses reject secularism in our pleasure.
4. What is your response to the author's personal testimony about his discovery and enjoyment of classical music? Explain.
5. Read Psalm 19. In what two ways does God reveal himself? Which is more important for our understanding of the other way? Explain.

* * *

One Step on Our Journey with Jesus: Pray persistently that God, through Jesus, will replace the secularism in your fun life with sacredness done for the 3-in-1 Creator God. As he gives you victory through Jesus over Satan's secular influence, tell other people near you, giving him the credit.

* * *

**While we creep toward God's final kingdom,
let's look at our responses to the...**

Chapter Thirteen

WEATHER

Weather and its effects dragging our emotions down

I woke up one morning in the long, frigid, West Michigan winter of 2013-2014 to a beautiful sunny day with the beauty of the new Alberta-Clipper and Lake-Michigan-effect snow. It was God's creative beauty in a long, difficult winter. However, according to my scientific weather station, last night's low temperature was zero degrees Fahrenheit. And then the temperature rose to a "balmy" seven degrees above zero Fahrenheit in the morning.

How can we learn to enjoy God in every kind of weather?

When I was a boy on the farm, I loved cloudy and rainy days in the summer. Why? Well, on those days, I didn't have to work. I hated farmwork and was bored with the farm. I just wasn't a farm boy at heart.

At any rate, we've lived four times in the West Michigan area in a county next to Lake Michigan, which God uses to bring us many cloudy days in wintertime. However, I have never minded cloudy days because of my farm experience.

Why do people hate the cloudy weather, especially so much of it in the winter? It's hard for me to understand why people get depressed because it's cloudy.

I know that some people have the condition called SAD, seasonal affective disorder. Mayo Clinic's website says about that disease, "Seasonal affective disorder (also called SAD) is a type of depression that occurs at the same time every year. If you're like most people with seasonal affective disorder, your symptoms start in the fall and may continue into the winter months, sapping your energy and making you feel moody. Less often, seasonal affective disorder causes depression in the spring or early summer. Treatment for seasonal affective disorder includes light therapy (phototherapy), psychotherapy, and medications."

My suggestion, like that of Mayo Clinic, is that you seek psychological help to find out the cause of your seasonal depression, since I suffered through seven years of depression. In my experience, it's important to face depression, find out what's causing it, and seek God's help through professional people as his means to help you overcome your depression. (See my first two books, *Doubtbusters! God Is My Shrink!* and *Be Bolder Growin' Older*.)

Dealing with the weather's effects on us

In addition, how can we deal with so many cloudy days in the winter and any time?

First, it seems to me that we are focusing on the clouds rather than on the light coming through the clouds, which don't make it pitch-black, the way God sent blackness to the Egyptians as one of the plagues to set Israel free. Someone said to me when I suggested that we could concentrate on the light, "No light comes through the clouds."

I pointed out to that person, "If that were true, we wouldn't be able to see anything. Some light enters our life with clouds, and we can be thankful for that fact."

Second, God sends clouds to provide moisture for the soil. Without rain and snow, nothing would grow, as we experienced in the Arizona Sonoran Desert in February 2012. We praised God for his creative power in giving the desert plants the ability to survive with only twelve inches of rain a year, mostly coming in June.

Third, God's Word has a lot to say about the weather. People say, "It rained" or "It snowed." What is "it"? I'm afraid that our secular culture has influenced us to separate God from the weather with such language.

On the other hand, the Prophet Jeremiah says, in contrast to the false gods of his day, "But God made the earth by his power; he founded the world by his wisdom and stretched out the heavens by his understanding. When he thunders, the waters in the heavens roar; he makes clouds rise from the ends of the earth. He sends lightning with the rain and brings out the wind from his storehouses" (Jeremiah 10:12–13).

Fourth, in the winter, God keeps our temperature in West Michigan up a few degrees when we experience his clouds. Also, he uses Lake Michigan to keep us from most of the intense, destructive tornadoes that the Midwest and Southwest experience much more often. The most powerful one in our area was about sixty years ago.

Fifth, when God allows the weather to be trying, we in our area and other parts of the world should consider the people elsewhere whose houses have been leveled by a tornado or hurricane. After all, most of us don't have it that bad.

A *Grand Rapids Press* article by religion-writer Charles Honey caught my eye when I was writing this chapter. The winter had turned to a spring that was still cooler than normal. He wrote under the headline "Springtime sun is balm for the soul." Curiously, he quoted Psalm 19:4c–6, verses that compare the sun to a bridegroom or champion racing across the heavens, without referring to God's showing of his great power through his creation. "The heavens declare the glory of God, the skies proclaim the work of his hands" (verse 1).

The writer then goes on to give us several tongue-in-cheek features of spring's arrival:

"How can we be sure it's spring? Let me count some of the ways:

* You actually want to go outside.
* Your heart feels lighter.

* You feel a certain giddiness, like the first time you wanted to kiss that kid on the playground.
* You feel a sudden urge to dig your hands in the dirt.
* The birds are singing, and you stop to listen to them.
* Opening day of baseball season has come.
* You walk around your yard and notice green things poking out of the ground."

Charles Honey concludes his article with these words: "Clearly spring's time had come. Time to rejoice and be a kid again." His article is an interesting secular approach to the weather even though he is the newspaper's religion editor.

Instead, I say that we can rejoice in the true God both in the dead of winter and in the return of life in spring. There's no question that we in a northern American climate really appreciate spring's arrival, since it contrasts with winter's bleakness.

I'm sure that if you live in a warmer climate than we have in West Michigan, you can think of other features of the weather that you dislike and some that you like. However, no perfect weather anywhere exists in between the Garden of Eden and the future new universe.

My point is that we question God when we get frustrated at the weather, especially when it's as cloudy, cold, and long as the winter was for many people. When we get frustrated with the weather, we are really frustrated with the God who allowed our struggle to enable us to look to him for relief.

God and bad weather

Of course, the Bible does say that Satan directly brings bad weather like tornadoes and hurricanes by God's permission for his people's good. In Job 1:18–19, a messenger reports to Job the ultimate disaster, suddenly, a mighty wind swept in from the desert and killed all of his ten children. We know by the previous scene in heaven that God gives Satan permission to test Job's faith but controls the extent of the devil's attacks on Job. "Very well, then, everything that he has is in your hands, but on the man himself do not lay a finger" (Job 1:12).

Thus, God is directly or indirectly involved in all events, including the weather. When he allows the cloudy days and weather that test our faith, he seeks our persistent prayers for perseverance and patience. When we fail those tests, we need to confess our self-centeredness and to continue to ask for his gifts of those character qualities that we lack and that he can use to enable us to get through a long, cloudy, and cold winter, as well as any bad weather.

Therefore, God calls us to praise him for all kinds of weather, even winter cloudiness, and to pray for his gift of spiritual growth to endure it and, yes, to rejoice in him as we experience his changes.

A paraphrase of the Bible to prove a point

Two pastors of Fairhaven Church of the town I live in—Hudsonville, Michigan, U.S.A.—wrote the following paraphrase of Philippians 4:10 and Ephesians 6:10–17 toward the end of the long, hard winter of 2013–2014 in West Michigan, during which we experienced the second most snow on record and broke many low-temperature records:

"(Philippians 4:10) I know what it is to be covered in the snow, and I know what it is to see the sun. I have learned the secret of being content in any and every situation, whether icy or sunny, whether windy with snow or on balmy beaches. I can do all this through him who gives me strength.... (Ephesians 6:10) Finally, be warm in the Lord and in his mighty power. [11]Put on the full snowmobile suit of God so that you can take your stand against the devil's storms. [12]For our struggle is not against slush and sleet, but against the spiritual polar vortexes, against the hopeless forecasts of this frigid world and against the spiritual forces of cold in the heavenly realms. [13]Therefore, put on the full snow gear of God, so that when the day of evil comes, you may be warm, and after you have done everything, to be warm. [14]Be warm, then, with the muffler of truth buckled around your waist, with the down vest of righteousness in place, [15]and with your feet fitted with the mukluks of the gospel of peace. [16]In addition to all this, take up the plastic sled of faith, with which you can bat away all the freezing snow balls of the evil one. [17]Take the stocking cap of salvation and the hockey stick of the Spirit, which is the word of God." — Pastor Tom Elenbaas and Pastor Scott VanArendonk of Fairhaven Church, Hudsonville, Michigan, U.S.A.

I believe that these pastors' point in making this paraphrase is that God can give us his power to endure harsh winters, bad weather, and any other adverse circumstance by giving us joyful contentment and the strength to battle the evil forces, who are the direct cause of the temptations we feel about bad weather.

In Philippians 4:10, Paul tells us that he is content in all circumstances. At the time of writing this letter to the believers in Philippi, he is under house arrest in Rome awaiting trial before fickle Emperor Nero, who could put him to death. How can he be content under those circumstances? Since Paul has suffered great opposition throughout his ministry, God teaches him that his emotional state is not dependent on his outward circumstances. Through constant prayer, he has learned to focus more and more on his 3-in-1 God and less and less on other people's responses to his ministry.

When we undergo the storms of life, including bad weather, we can learn from Paul's experiences that it is best to let God guide us rather than the weather.

In Ephesians 6:10–17, inspired Paul calls us to put on the whole armor of God. He uses the Roman soldier's outfit to illustrate the idea that if we are close to God and immersed in prayer and his Word, the Bible, the devil cannot influence our lives.

The next verse (Ephesians 6:18a) after the pastors' paraphrased passage, however, is the clincher, "And pray in the Spirit on all occasions with all kinds of prayers and requests." When we let the weather or anything get us down, God calls us through Paul to pray persistently to the Creator of the weather and other circumstances for relief. Thus, God wants us to "be bolder growin' older" in prayer to him about the weather and every other trying circumstance.

As a result, God wants us to express to him our frustrations that are caused by the weather. We must also pray for more contentment and strength to be his soldiers in the war against the evil forces that are tempting us to question God, our Creator. Prayer is his substitute for our complaints to others about our difficult circumstances.

The Creator of the weather and the Inspirer of the Book of Jonah

In addition, the book of Jonah helps us with our relationship to the weather. Of course, Jonah "runs away" from God's call to preach repentance to his people's archenemy, the city of Nineveh. He rebels against God by taking a ship that is supposed to head for the other end of the Mediterranean Sea, as far from Nineveh as he can go. The Bible says in Jonah 1:4, "Then the LORD sent a great wind on the sea, and such a violent wind arose that the ship threatened to break up." Some interpreters, who I suspect have been influenced by modern secularism, try to explain away God's involvement in the weather by saying that his sending the storm is merely a figure of speech.

However, we already know from the books of Job and Psalms that God rules all of his creation. He probably allows Satan, as in Job chapters 1 and 2, to send the storm. However, it's all part of his plan to discipline his rebellious prophet Jonah for his good.

The two good results are the sailors' faith and repentance as well as Jonah's redirected will to preach in Nineveh, though reluctantly. God brings the latter result about in Jonah 2:10, "But the LORD provided a great fish to swallow Jonah." After Jonah's prayer of praise for God's rescue from his drowning, the LORD commands the fish to vomit Jonah onto dry land.

A note is necessary about Jonah's huge fish experience. Many people, influenced by rationalism, the attempt to reason everything out, and naturalism, the idea that nothing supernatural happens in nature, have charged that this incident is impossible.

However, Jesus confirms that God rescued Jonah from the sea through a huge fish, not a whale, in Matthew 12:40. After saying that his generation always needs a miraculous sign from Jesus to demonstrate that he is from God, he responds, "But none will be given [this generation] except the sign of the prophet Jonah. For as Jonah was three days and three nights in the belly of a huge fish, so the Son of Man will be three days and three nights in the heart of the earth."

In this passage, Jesus confirms the facts that Jonah's experience actually happened, that it was a miracle, and that God's rescue of Jonah looks forward to Jesus' actual death on a cross for God's forgiveness. Jonah's experience also anticipates Jesus' actual resurrection from death to give us resurrection life, beginning now and completed at his Second Coming.

Not only does the Creator of the wind and fish make them, but he also guides all of nature. He is all-powerful in disciplining his wayward children who tend to separate him from his creation. However, his will to allow the cold winters of our lives is always for our good, to teach us his lessons. The sad thing is that we fail to learn from his storms because of secular thinking.

Jesus and the weather

Another Bible passage emphasizing Jesus' divine control of the weather as well as his followers' unbelief is Mark 4:35–41. Jesus leads his disciples out onto the Sea of Galilee in the evening, when rain squalls often occur. His fishermen followers, who normally work third-shift through the night to catch fish, not in the dangerous evening, wake him in the middle of a sudden storm that threatens to swamp the boat. Then Jesus "got up, rebuked the wind, and said to the waves, 'Quiet! Be still!' Then, the wind died down and the weather was completely still. He said to his disciples, 'Why are you afraid? Do you still have no faith?'"

If we let the weather affect our moods by frustrating and even frightening us, we are like Jesus' disciples who later become pillars of the church. However, they, like us, have to learn to focus on Jesus, the Agent of our heavenly Father, in ruling the weather and everything else in his creation.

The Gospel of Mark emphasizes the unbelief of Jesus' chosen men to comfort the non-Jewish people to whom Mark writes his Good News, since they have to face severe persecution for their faith. The next verse (41) shows his followers' lack of insight into Jesus' divine nature. "They were terrified and asked each other, 'Who is this? Even the wind and the waves obey him?'"

That crucial question confronts every human, "Who is Jesus?" How we answer it makes all the difference in this life and the next. He is the God-man with all-power to deliver us.

Bible Discussion Questions:

1. What kinds of weather get Christians down? Why? What do you think about the author's suggestions for dealing with the weather under the heading "Dealing with the weather's effects on us"? Explain your reaction.
2. Read Job 1:12–19. What is your reaction to the fact that God allows Satan to kill Job's ten children with a desert tornado? Read Job 1:20–22. With what three actions does Job respond to the horrible loss of his children? Why do all three actions receive the response of verse 22? Explain.
3. What is your reaction to the two pastors' paraphrase of the Philippians and Ephesians passages in terms of a long, cold winter? How can God help you deal with all kinds of weather? Explain.
4. How do Jonah's experiences with the wind and the huge fish and their parallel with Jesus' death and resurrection help you overcome hard experiences with the weather and other difficulties? Explain.
5. Read Mark 4:35–41. How does Jesus' divine mastery of the storm comfort you in the face of bad weather and other circumstances? Explain.

* * *

One Step on Our Journey with Jesus: If you have been separating God from the weather, thank him for

his blessing when he gives you good weather, and pray for his guidance for your spiritual growth during bad weather and other difficult circumstances. Pray for the ability to focus on God's good divine nature and blessings rather than on your environment. Share God's victory with other people as Jesus gives it to you.

* * *

Nearing our final goal of resurrection perfection, we gaze upon our Maker-Rescuer in...

Chapter Fourteen

GROUP WORSHIP

God's pleasure and will for our worship of him

I once talked to a young man whom God saved during an exciting young people's worship service. He said that he was leaving our church for another one with a freer worship style. His reason was that he wanted to have the same feeling in church that he had when God rescued him. I said that I understood his decision, but I have often thought about his reason for leaving our church.

It now occurs to me that to get a certain feeling of joy in worship is not a good excuse to leave a church. After all, why do we go to church at all? Is it to recapture some past experience for our pleasure, or is it to use our intellect, feelings, and will to honor God? Is worship's purpose to get from God or to give to him?

God, in his Word, the Bible, has a lot to say about group worship. He supplies many calls to worship in his book through his inspired writers.

Once, I asked an over-the-road trucker why he didn't go to church. He replied, "I can feel just as close to God and can worship him just as well walking out in the woods." In response, I shared with him some of the following Bible passages about group worship.

In Psalm 95:1–7, the inspired writer calls us, "Come, let us sing for joy to the LORD; let us shout aloud to the Rock of our salvation. Let us come before him with thanksgiving and extol him with music and song. For the LORD is the great God, the great King above all gods. In his hand are the depths of the earth, and the mountain peaks belong to him. The sea is his, for he made it, and his hands formed the dry land. Come, let us bow down in worship; let us kneel before the LORD our Maker; for he is our God and we are the people of his pasture, the flock under his care."

This passage not only calls us to worship God joyfully with other believers, but it also gives us the reason, because God is the only true Creator of the universe and the Deliverer of his true followers.

Someone might ask why God requires us to worship him. Isn't he being selfish? The answer is that the 3-in-1 God is the only one worthy of human worship.

We talk about celebrity worship, but no singers, movie stars, or sports personalities are worthy of our worship, because they are fallible, imperfect humans. Only God is the perfect Creator of all humans. He is the only one to whom we owe our praise. He's God and we're not.

A New Testament passage emphasizing our worship with other believers is Hebrews 10:25, among other verses calling us to be mutually accountable to each other. "Let us not give up meeting together, as some are in the habit of doing, but let us encourage one another—all the more as you see the Day approaching." The words "meeting together" translate a specific Greek word for group worship of God with other believers. However, we don't worship God because he requires it in this verse, but because we want to refocus our lives on him in gratitude for his loving actions in Jesus.

Also, as we see Jesus' return coming closer, we need to make worshipping with other believers a high priority every time. (See chapter 10 in *Doubtbusters! God Is My Shrink!*)

Another passage is Jeremiah 32:40–41, in which God promises to return Israel to the Promised Land. "I will make an everlasting covenant with them: I will never stop doing good to them, and I will inspire them to fear me, so that they will never turn away from me. I will rejoice in doing them good and will assuredly plant them in this land with all my heart and soul."

(1) Notice that God's emphasis is on his covenant relationship with his people as a group, not just as individuals.
(2) Our relationship with the LORD as a group of believers is the object of his pleasure.
(3) Our worship grows out of our faith connection with the true God of the Bible, not the feelings we get out of worship and service, though such feelings naturally result from our worship.

(4) Since we often have imperfect lives with mixed motives, I contend that the only way God is pleased with our fallen worship and works is because of God's acceptance of Jesus' perfection in his life, death, and resurrection.

(5) God uses the Persian king Cyrus to return Israel to Palestine, but they replace their idols with trust in the Law and their many rules to try to please God. Because they reject and crucify Jesus as the promised Messiah, God establishes the international church, instead of national Israel, to be his worshipers, even predicting that change, a new form of the covenant God made with Abraham, in Jeremiah 31:31–34.

(6) Jesus' discussion with the Samaritan woman in John chapter 4 emphatically shows that "God is spirit, and his worshipers must worship him in spirit and in truth" (verse 24).

(7) My whole point is that worship does not depend on a certain worship style or some emotional reaction that we get from it, but on our giving our whole being to God. All of life is worship. Therefore, our group worship is an extension of that personal relationship or covenant with him that prepares us to honor God in all of life.

Two more Bible passages about our worship

In Psalm 50, God doesn't condemn his people for their animal sacrifices, but for those offerings made with wicked motives. Then, in verses 14 and 15, God gives us his call for our genuine worship: "Sacrifice thank offerings to God, fulfill your vows to the Most High, and call upon me in the day of trouble; I will deliver you, and you will honor me."

Thus, thanksgiving for Jesus Christ's substitution for us on the cross and his resurrection is the basic motive for our meeting with God as worshipers in a group.

Another relevant Old Testament passage is Isaiah 58:13–14: After condemning hypocritical religious observances like fasting that don't reflect his gift of changed lives, God—through Isaiah—says, "If you keep your feet from breaking the Sabbath and from doing as you please on my holy day, if you call the Sabbath a delight and the LORD's holy day honorable, and if you honor it by not going your own way and not doing as you please or speaking idle words, then you will find your joy in the LORD, and I will cause you to ride on the heights of the land and to feast on the inheritance of your father Jacob. The mouth of the LORD has spoken."

We need to sort out the old covenant parts of this passage from the important principles that God wants us new covenant believers to learn and apply to our lives.

(1) Israel's Sabbath-day form disappears when Jesus dies on the cross (Colossians 2:16–17).

(2) Worshiping God on the day when his people gather is never a duty. God wants us to give one day in seven to him for rest and worship with great delight and joy, whether our outward celebration shows it or not.

(3) How much greater joy do Christians have to celebrate Jesus Christ's conception and birth as the God-baby; his perfect life as the God-man; his agonizing death as our perfect, willing

Substitute; and his powerful, permanent resurrection to give us eternal triumph? That joy can come in any style of worship with content that is true to God's Word, the Bible.

(4) God promises to bless us abundantly because we rejoice in him with his people once a week.

(5) On a personal note, I'm enjoying resting and worshiping with God's people one day a week, whereas when I was preaching God's Word for twenty-seven years, I worshiped with them but certainly didn't rest on the day of worship. Instead, I rested on Monday.

(6) We need to give a whole day to God as his way to "recharge our spiritual batteries." I'm thankful that our church still has two different worship services, morning and evening, for a double Lord's Day blessing of responding to his proclaimed Word.

(7) God wants that day every week to be his training ground for our individual worship the other days of the week, including our times of pleasure. I also use that day for praising the Creator for his creation of the human body in TV sports while I talk with our children and grandchildren.

Now, we reflect on some church humor from jokes.ochristian.com:

A little girl was in church with her mother when she started feeling ill. "Mommy," she said, "can we leave now?"

"No," her mother replied.

"Well, I think I'm gonna be sick, Momma!"

"Then go out the front door and around to the back of the church and then behind a bush."

After about 60 seconds the little girl returned to her seat.

"Were you sick?" her mom asked.

"Yes."

"How could you have gone all the way to the back of the church and returned so quickly?"

"I didn't have to go out of the church, Mommy. They have a box next to the front door that says, 'For the Sick.'"

After describing his great travels, the $20 dollar bill asked the $1 dollar bill, "What about you? Where have you been?"

The $1 dollar bill replied, "Well, I've been to the Baptist church, the Methodist church, the Presbyterian church, the Episcopalian church, the Church of God in Christ, the Catholic church, the Mormon church, the church of the Latter Day Saints, the A.M.E. church, the Disciple of Christ church, the…"

"WAIT A MINUTE! WAIT A MINUTE!!" shouted the $20 dollar bill to the $1 dollar bill. "What's a church??"

An old priest was getting sick and tired of all the people in his parish who kept confessing adultery. One Sunday in the pulpit he said, "If I hear one more person confess to adultery, I'll quit!"

Everyone liked him, so the parishioners came up with a code word. Someone who had committed adultery would say they had "fallen." This seemed to satisfy the old priest and things went well, until the priest died at a ripe old age.

About a week later, the new priest visited the Mayor of the town and seemed very concerned. The priest said, "You have to do something about the sidewalks in town. When people come into the confessional, they keep talking about having fallen."

The Mayor started to laugh, realizing that no one had told the new priest about the code word.

The priest shook an accusing finger at the mayor and said, "I don't know what you're laughing about. Your wife fell three times this week."

Bible Discussion Questions:

1. Read Psalm 95:1–7. Why does God have to inspire the biblical writers to call us to worship him with his people? Why do you think we should worship God with his people weekly? What should be our motive for gathering with God's church to praise, pray, give, and to receive God's shared Word? Explain.

2. Read Hebrews 10:25 in its context. Why does God call us to worship with other Christians in this verse? For what purpose? What other purposes does God accept? Explain.

3. Read Jeremiah 32:40–41. Which ones of the author's seven explanations touch your life the most? Why?

4. Read Psalm 50:14–15 and Isaiah 58:14–15. In what ways are the old and new covenants different in the way they approach the day of worship? How are they the same? What main ideas do they both have in common? Explain.

5. How do you celebrate the day set aside for worship and rest? How might your approach change as a result of this Bible study? Explain.

* * *

One Step on Our Journey with Jesus: Make a conscious decision with your family to set aside the day when the people of God meet for worship as a day of rest and worship, not one of rules. Dedicate that day to the 3-in-1 God of the Bible and attend worship every time your church worships. Pray for him to give you the right motives and actions on that day that will please him in his strength through Jesus.

* * *

Final Part: Jesus' path to God without hedonism, separatism, modernism, or secularism

As I drove through Chicago coming home from two graduations, I saw a billboard ad for "GooglePlay," which had the slogan "Play Your Heart Out." My suggestion to you would rather be, "Play with all of your heart with Jesus' joy."

I hope that in your reading and/or discussing of this book, the 3-in-1 God has given you more of his victory through Jesus Christ over any influences from secularism (separating God from fun) or hedonism (pursuing fun for its own sake). I also hope that you too will be able to interpret and apply God's Word for your pleasurable activities in order to give them to God.

Finally, I hope that you can find God's middle way of honoring him with pleasure in which you can be involved with a good conscience instead of separatism (separating completely from our culture) or modernism (unthinkingly blending in with our culture's fun-loving).

Now, we have come to the end of this second leg of our journey with Jesus during the "Step-By-Step Series." I hope that you had God's fun discovering how to experience pleasure dedicated to praising and honoring him. May God bless all of your pleasurable activities with the joy of Jesus!